TRUE CRIME AND
THE JUSTICE OF GOD

TRUE CRIME AND THE JUSTICE OF GOD

Ethics, Media, and Forensic Science

Elisabeth T. Vasko and Lyndsie Ferrara

ORBIS BOOKS
Maryknoll, New York 10545

Founded in 1970, Orbis Books endeavors to publish works that enlighten the mind, nourish the spirit, and challenge the conscience. The publishing arm of the Maryknoll Fathers and Brothers, Orbis seeks to explore the global dimensions of the Christian faith and mission, to invite dialogue with diverse cultures and religious traditions, and to serve the cause of reconciliation and peace. The books published reflect the views of their authors and do not represent the official position of the Maryknoll Society. To learn more about Maryknoll and Orbis Books, please visit our website at www.orbisbooks.com.

Manufactured in the United States of America.
Manuscript editing and typesetting by Joan Weber Laflamme.

Library of Congress Cataloging-in-Publication Data

Names: Vasko, Elisabeth T., author. | Ferrara, Lyndsie, author.
Title: True crime and the justice of God : ethics, media, and forensic science / Elisabeth T. Vasko and Lyndsie Ferrara.
Description: Maryknoll, NY : Orbis Books, [2022] | Includes bibliographical references and index. | Summary: "Utilizing the tools of forensic science and Christian theological ethics, this book resituates prominent criminal cases within their social and forensic contexts"— Provided by publisher.
Identifiers: LCCN 2021036259 (print) | LCCN 2021036260 (ebook) | ISBN 9781626984721 (trade paperback) | ISBN 9781608339341 (epub)
Subjects: LCSH: Equality—Religious aspects—Catholic Church.
Classification: LCC BX1795.J87 V37 2022 (print) | LCC BX1795.J87 (ebook) | DDC 261.8—dc23
LC record available at https://lccn.loc.gov/2021036259
LC ebook record available at https://lccn.loc.gov/2021036260

FOR ELISE

FOR MICHAEL

CONTENTS

INTRODUCTION

There's a saying in the media: "If it bleeds, it leads." The more grotesque, the more sensational the story, the greater the coverage. The goal of the media is to sell stories. While a number of factors influence the stories that make it to the "top of the hour" or the front page, many Americans say that they watch true crime as a form of entertainment.[1] Podcasts like *Serial* have reached almost half a billion downloads.[2] Today, true crime can be found on nearly every major television network, from *Forensic Files* on Amazon Prime to Oxygen's *Snapped*. ID (previously Investigation Discovery) is a television network exclusively focused on around-the-clock retelling of heinous criminal activity. In 2019, the New York Police Department (NYPD) even jumped on the bandwagon, producing and releasing its own true crime podcast, *Break in the Case*. True crime is a multibillion-dollar industry in the United States. There are over twenty-eight-hundred podcasts, and ad revenue in 2018 was $479 million.[3] True crime conventions like *CrimeCon* sell out months in advance. True crime junkies wear shirts that read "Murder Shows and Comfy

---

[1] Kelly Leigh-Cooper, "Is Our Growing Obsession with True Crime a Problem?" *BBC Wisconsin*, April 1, 2019.

[2] Todd Spangler, "'Serial' Season 3 Podcast Premiere Date Set," *Variety*, Sept 5, 2018.

[3] See Melissa Chan, "Real People Keep Getting Re-traumatized: The Human Cost of Binge-Watching True Crime Series," *Time,* April 24, 2020.

Clothes." True crime is cathartic for people. The question is
why, and what does it say about us? Why is there such an "easy
acceptance of murder as entertainment?"[4]

By and large, true crime media is targeted toward white wom-
en.[5] Production companies and mass marketing consider what
appeals to white women in deciding whose stories to feature
and how to tell them. True crime is participatory media in the
sense that streaming services and social media normalize spec-
tators to search for clues and seek out evidence. Journalist and
true crime junkie Rachel Monroe says that women "speculate
about unsolved crimes—and sometimes solve them—and you'll
find that most of the posters are women. More than seven in
ten students of forensic science, one of the fastest-growing college majors, are women."[6] Many consumers describe true crime
as comforting. Monroe recounts a conversation with staff at
Oxygen: "If you look at the ratings for Investigation Discovery
(Oxygen's true crime programming rival), he told me, they're
the same at midnight as they are at 6:00 a.m. 'People leave it on
all night,' he said. 'They fall asleep to it. People tell me all the
time that they find these shows soothing.'"[7] What is behind the
obsession? While some researchers posit a desire to learn about
survival and crime to avoid becoming victims themselves, others
suggest voyeurism and a fascination with evil.[8] So why does true
crime matter for Christian ethics?

---

[4] Jean Murley, *The Rise of True Crime: 20th Century Murder and American Popular Culture* (Westport, CT: Praeger, 2008), 2.

[5] See Michelle Harven, "Investigating Our Obsession with True Crime Podcasts," *NPR*, February 8, 2021.

[6] Rachel Monroe, *Savage Appetites: Four True Stories of Women, Crime, and Obsession* (New York: Scribner, 2019), Kindle edition, 4.

[7] Ibid., 6–7.

[8] Amanda M. Vicary and R. Chris Fraley, "Captured by True Crime: Why Are Women Drawn to Tales of Rape, Murder, and Serial Killers?" *Social Psychological and Personality Science* 1, no. 1 (2010): 81–86. Questions about voyeurism, the carceral state, race, and gender are complex. (The term *carceral state* refers

While true crime media may be targeted toward white women, it plays a significant role in the racialization of crime and justice the United States. *Racialization* is a term that sociologists use to describe how racial and ethnic meaning are socially and historically constructed and disseminated in society.[9] Racialization occurs at both the macro and micro levels; within minoritized communities, across minoritized communities, and between minoritized communities and whites, albeit to different degrees.[10] At the macro level, racialization can be seen in Western imperialism, chattel slavery, and accompanying economic, sociocultural, and religious structures. On a smaller scale, racialization can be seen in racial profiling.[11] Sociologists Michael Omi and Howard Winant, whose work informs our discussion here, understand race as a master category. This means that race informs our interpretation of other categories like gender, work, innocence, guilt, victim, survivor, and even God. In the United States, media plays a critical role in racial formation. As we illustrate in this book, the majority of modern true crime stories interpret violence in a way that desensitizes the public to systemic gendered and racial inequities in society. A variety of factors contribute to this, some of which include fictional representations and perpetrator/victim binaries.

True crime focuses on the storytelling by making the crimes exciting and entertaining to viewers while often forgetting the

---

to the various ways that the logic of surveillance, control, and criminalization shapes society.) From welfare to public housing, the carceral state reaches far beyond prison itself. For more on this topic, see Kaaryn S. Gustafson, *Cheating Welfare: Public Assistance and the Criminalization of Poverty* (New York: NYU Press, 2012). Also see University of Michigan Research Institute, "Carceral State Project: Documenting Criminalization and Confinement from the University of Michigan," https://sites.lsa.umich.edu/dcc-project/.

[9] Michael Omi and Howard Winant, *Racial Formation in the United States*, 3rd ed. (New York: Routledge, 2015), Kindle edition, 111.

[10] Ibid., 105ff.

[11] Ibid., 111–12.

humanity of the people and communities affected. This is a serious moral problem to which many viewers are oblivious. For example, what does it mean for white women to claim that true crime is cathartic when BIPOC (Black, Indigenous, People of Color) are repeatedly depicted as bestial, animalistic, and dangerous? What does such praxis signify in a country that is the world leader in incarceration per capita?[12] What kind of moral response does true crime media endorse? How do Western Christian religious ideals about sin, purity, and innocence intersect with those presented in true crime media? These are questions that tap into the heart of one of the most pressing moral problems today: white supremacy and anti-Blackness.

In her prophetic text *Stand Your Ground: Black Bodies and the Justice of God*, womanist theologian Kelly Brown Douglas illustrates the death-dealing powers of Manifest Destiny and Anglo-Saxon exceptionalism, narratives that have weaponized the Christian faith.[13] For Douglas, the justice of God is linked to human freedom and human dignity. She writes: "God's power respects the integrity of all human bodies and the sanctity of all life. This is a resurrecting power. Therefore, God's power never expresses itself through the humiliation or denigration of another."[14] Salvation is liberation. One small part of this work is "naming and calling out the very narratives, ideologies, and discourses of power that indeed promote the culture of stand-your-ground sin . . . and going to the root."[15] This would include media images, which are powerful conveyers of meaning in contemporary society.

Media images help shape our view of the world, what we perceive as good, evil, and beautiful. While the relationship

---

[12] See https://www.sentencingproject.org/criminal-justice-facts.

[13] Kelly Brown Douglas, *Stand Your Ground: Black Bodies and the Justice of God* (Maryknoll, NY: Orbis Books, 2015), 127, 187.

[14] Ibid., 183.

[15] Ibid., 196.

between television viewing and political attitudes is not always directly correlated or causal, communication scholars have determined that the influence of media increases as the public's direct experience with a social issue decreases. In particular, those who study cultivation theory have observed that "information communicated to viewers via media like television can influence the audience's perception of social reality in a subtle and cumulative fashion."[16] Entertainment crime media has a priming effect, foregrounding the problem of violent crime in the eyes of the viewer, especially for those who watch regularly.

Ongoing research within the fields of communication and criminology reveal complex relationships between crime representations (real and fictional) and the influence of crime media on the ideas/attitudes of viewers.[17] Research indicates that media representations of crime inflate viewer beliefs regarding crime rates and the violent nature of crimes.[18] Heinous crimes have been used to appeal to the public and to push specific political agendas.[19] Such trends are particularly troubling in view of true crime media for several reasons. First, entertainment sources are "often treated as inconsequential to the formation of political attitudes."[20] Members of the general public rarely stop to reflect critically upon entertainment sources, especially

---

[16] Johanna Blakley and Sheena Nahm, "MCD: Primetime War on Terror," The Norman Lear Center, ACLU & USC, May 15, 2017.

[17] Aaron Doyle, "How Not to Think about Crime in the Media," *Canadian Journal of Criminology and Criminal Justice* 48, no. 6 (2006): 867–85.

[18] See Andrew J. Baranauskas and Kevin M. Drakulich, "Media Construction of Crime Revisited: Media Types, Consumer Contexts, and Frames of Crime and Justice," *Criminology* 54, no. 4 (2018): 681.

[19] Ken Dowler, Thomas Fleming, and Stephen L. Muzzatti, "Constructing Crime: Media, Crime, and Popular Culture," *Canadian Journal of Criminology and Criminal Justice* 48, no. 6 (2006): 837–50.

[20] See R. Andrew Holbrook and Timothy G. Hill, "Agenda-Setting and Priming in Prime-Time Television: Crime Dramas as Political Cues," *Political Communication* 22, no. 3 (2005): 78.

those considered to be sensationalized.[21] This is a problem given the sheer amount of time spent on phones, tablets, and other devices. Second, as we discuss further in Chapters 1 and 2, true crime distorts patterns of crime in America, highlighting mainly cases of white women who are victims of violent crimes. This is a skewed representation of American crime, as it ignores white-collar offenses and nonviolent crime and "contributes to the wide-spread belief that the American murder problem is limited to white, middle-class sexual predators or domestic violence-related attacks."[22]

This book argues that true crime interprets violence in a way that desensitizes the public to gendered and racial inequities in society, thereby constricting and contorting the moral imagination. As Douglas writes, "A moral imagination is grounded in the absolute belief that the world can be better. . . . It is not constrained by what is. It is oriented toward what will be."[23] For Christians, the moral imagination represents a call to disrupt, interrupt, and transform spaces that fail to reflect God's intention for all living beings to have life. Christians are called to live as if God's "kin-dom" is already, even though in many spaces it is "not yet." We are not called to lives of complacency in the face of violence. True crime normalizes injustice through its easy

---

[21] Joy Wiltenburg makes this point in "True Crime: The Origins of Modern Sensationalism," *American Historical Review* 109, no. 5 (2004): 1378.

[22] Murley, *The Rise of True Crime*, 121. The 2019 expanded homicide data from the Federal Bureau of Investigation (FBI) Uniform Crime Reporting Program denotes a higher number of Black victims (54.7 percent) and offenders (55.9 percent) when race was known. Additionally, 53.7 percent of total murder victims were Black males. It is important to note that the data provided is based on the law enforcement agencies that choose to submit information to the FBI program. The terms *victim* and *offender* are used in the report. US Department of Justice, Federal Bureau of Investigation, Criminal Justice Information Services Division, "Expanded Homicide," *2019 Crime in the United States* (September 2019).

[23] Douglas, *Stand Your Ground*, 225.

acceptance of violence as entertainment, the sensationalism of violence against women, and the reification of whiteness.[24]

In this coauthored book, Lyndsie and I examine the cultural, scientific, religious, and moral effects of true crime media. As a forensic scientist and educator, Lyndsie wrestles with some of the larger moral questions posed by the discipline of forensic science. While she situates criminal cases within a forensic context, her goal is not to provide the reader with the tools to do the work of solving criminal cases. Instead, Lyndsie dispels some of the scientific myths presented in true crime. As a theologian, I wrestle with the cultural, religious, and moral effects of true crime. While neither of us has all the answers, our hope is that readers will gain the necessary skills to question critically the vision of truth, reality, and justice that they see and hear in true crime media. In other words, we see media literacy as a critical moral praxis for moving toward justice.[25] As Christian ethicist Kate Ott notes, literacy is not just about learning how to use a language or tool; it also involves "the ability to creatively engage in particular social practices, to assume appropriate identities, and to form and maintain various social relationships."[26] Literacy must be supported by critical awareness of oneself and positionality in the world as well as a keen desire to learn about social systems and how they work in daily life. We hope that this book emboldens and enlivens within readers an expansive understanding of what justice can look like in their own communities. It is not enough to simply think outside of the box—we have to *live* outside of it.

To our white readers: you are likely to find your whiteness on display in ways that are uncomfortable. This is okay. We encourage you to sit with the discomfort. It is normal for white people to be uncomfortable as we unearth anti-Blackness, white

---

[24] Murley, *The Rise of True Crime*, 7.

[25] Kate Ott, *Christian Ethics in a Digital Society* (Lanham, MD: Rowman & Littlefield, 2018).

[26] Ibid., 9.

supremacy, or racism, and as we engage in racial justice work in a racist society. As white people, this is something that Lyndsie and I are still working on ourselves. White people, many of whom are Christian, have a responsibility to pay attention to the larger cultural forces at work. Media imagery, on the screen and in the form of podcasts, is a tremendously powerful force in society. It can be used to embolden and expand the moral imagination as we collectively work to create a more just and humane society; it can also dehumanize, traumatize, and strip people of human dignity. Christians affirm a God of freedom and justice, who sees all life as endowed with dignity.

INTENDED AUDIENCE

We write this book for fans of true crime, for Christian believers, and for those interested in the intersection of Christian ethics, media, and science. While there are times that we speak directly to white people, our goal is to open up a larger conversation among people of all backgrounds on the representation of crime and justice in media.[27] We also recognize that this book is limited in its perspective and that greater conversation is needed on the topic. We deeply regret not being able to focus on all of the cases or areas deserving of urgent attention in view of this topic, such as immigration, transgender sex work, and hate crimes. There is a vast amount of true crime media, and we hope that others will join us in the conversation.

This book is also for students, professors, and members of the larger community who wish to further engage questions of Christian ethics, science, and popular culture. We believe that theology and science are for everyone. We have done our best to keep the language accessible and to explain key concepts

---

[27] Karen Teel, "Can We Hear Him Now? James Cone's Enduring Challenge to White Theologians," *Theological Studies* 81, no. 3 (2020): 584.

and terms in plain language. While theology is an academic discipline, it is also what ordinary people do as they try to make sense out of the Christian story. In particular, theology is what people of faith "do when they try to think through the practical applications of their beliefs" in the modern world.[28] In today's context, a significant application of Christianity is in streaming and entertainment media.

Moreover, in Christian theology and ethics, being and doing are related. Ethics asks two interrelated questions: Who should I become, and What should I do? Christian ethics seeks to answer these questions in relation to God and the history of the Christian community. "What does God require each of us to be and act in a way that promotes Christian values in all that we do?"[29] Questions of being and doing are intrinsically related because our personal and collective identities inform how we live our daily lives. Concretely, what we value as important shapes the decisions we make (or fail to make) about the allocation of resources, such as time, money, or our emotional and spiritual energies.

What you do with your time matters. This does not mean that the purpose (telos) of life is to be as efficient as possible. (In fact, I suspect that trying to be efficient or productive every waking hour would not be fulfilling.) Instead, what you do matters because it shapes who you are. This is true not only in a pragmatic sense, but also in the sense of self-development and communal agency.

This being said, your social history, context, and identity will inform both the way you read this text and the way you interpret true crime. Throughout history, people from dominant social groups have not been attentive to how their own social identity informs interpretation. Toward this end, we wish to underscore a

---

[28] Laurel C. Schneider and Stephen G. Ray Jr., eds., *Awake to the Moment: An Introduction to Theology* (Louisville, KY: Westminster John Knox, 2016), 2.

[29] Ott, *Christian Ethics*, 3.

few key terms, assumptions, and phrases that are frequently used throughout the book.

KEY TERMS AND ASSUMPTIONS

At the outset, it is important to clearly state that Lyndsie and I identify as white, cis-gendered women. While we bring different life experiences to the conversation, we have more in common than we have differences. This is the case for many white people, despite our reluctance to acknowledge such similarities. Our differences in training (science v. humanities) are relatively inconsequential when you consider the history of racial segregation that marks the landscape of this country. As we have been working on this project, many people have asked how it was possible for us to collaborate across such a stark disciplinary divide. The answer is that we are both white women. As will be evident from the conversation in this book, Lyndsie and I do not agree on everything. Indeed, the sustained cross-disciplinary moral conversation we had and continue to have is integral to the book's methodology.

Throughout this process Lyndsie and I have been writing together and apart. We both contributed to the background research, collaboratively laid out the structure of the book, chose true crime media cases to feature, and gave input on chapter layouts. We did, however, make specific contributions to chapters according to our areas of expertise. Lyndsie brought her forensic expertise to Chapters 3 and 6. I took the lead in writing Chapters 2, 4, and 7. Chapters 1 and 5 were a collaborative effort. It is worth noting that this book would not be possible without the contribution of each party. Toward this end we have made some compromises in definition and method. We have also learned a great deal from one another. It is also worth noting that the primary use of the first-person plural is in direct reference to the coauthors of this book. In all other instances we have done our best to specify the "we" to whom Lyndsie and I are referring.

Finally, this book intentionally challenges the use of the terms *perpetrator* and *victim* within literature on moral theology and forensic science. In keeping with common practice in discourse on sexual violence, we refer to those who have experienced sexual trauma as *survivors* or *victim-survivors*. The purpose of this usage is to retain the agency of those who have been harmed. Sexual violation, while deeply traumatizing, does not define a person's humanity. Those whose assault was also part of a homicide, we refer to as *victims*. In a parallel vein we follow the lead of lawyer and founder of the Equal Justice Initiative, Bryan Stevenson, and believe that "each of us is more than the worst thing we've ever done."[30] People who have been convicted of crimes are not defined by those crimes. They are not robbers, murderers, perpetrators, or killers. They are human beings who committed murder. As people who have been convicted of crimes can also be victimized by the carceral system and are often defined by the system, we use the term *returning citizen* to refer to persons who have been incarcerated, irrespective of sentencing or the nature of conviction. This term, while imperfect, foregrounds the challenges of reentry and the rights to full citizenship of the person.[31] We refer to those currently embedded within the criminal justice system on account charges as a *person/people who are incarcerated*. Terms such as *perpetrator, offender,* and *inmate* are dehumanizing and stigmatizing, reducing a human being to a crime.[32] Labels can have longstanding effects; they can persuade us to forget that all people bear the imprint and likeness of God.

---

[30] Bryan Stevenson, *Just Mercy: A Story of Justice and Redemption* (New York: One World, 2015), 17–18.

[31] We borrow the term *returning citizen* from the Elsinore-Bennu Think Tank for Restorative Justice.

[32] There are a few places where terms like *perpetrator* or *killer* remain because it is necessary for content.

Stevenson reminds us that we all need a little mercy now and then.[33] For this reason we choose to use person-first language.[34] We realize that it is clunky, but it stands as a poignant reminder that those who are incarcerated are, first and foremost, human beings created *imago dei*.

While Christian ethics holds that actions (what we do) and identity (who we are) are intertwined, identity is always defined in relationship to God. One must never forget that at the very center of the Christian religion is Jesus Christ, a person who was executed as a criminal. The members of the first Christian community were onlookers to the execution of a criminal (Mk 15:21–40). They believed him. All Christians, especially white people in the United States, are called to rethink their own beliefs in view of how the criminal justice system defines life and death today. What does it mean to believe women? What does it mean to believe those who are incarcerated? What does it mean to believe in one another? What does it mean to believe in God's promises? This is the work we need to do, together.

BOOK OVERVIEW

Chapter 1 offers an introduction to the development of true crime, beginning with execution sermons and continuing to contemporary true crime streaming media, and situates the topic in relation to Christian ethics. Chapters 2 through 4 examine true crime and sexual violence. The vast majority of people continue to misconstrue sexual violence as the act of "bad" or pathological strangers. This myth tricks Christians into believing that violence could never happen to them and that they would never do anything so horrible. As the forensic evidence shows, this belief system is particularly pernicious with respect to sexual

---

[33] Stevenson, *Just Mercy*, 18.

[34] Akiba Solomon, "What Words We Use—and Avoid—When Covering People and Incarceration," *The Marshall Project*, April 12, 2021.

violence. Chapter 2 takes a closer look at the case of serial rapist/murderer Ted Bundy, along with the Steubenville, Ohio, rape case featured in *Roll Red Roll* (2019). The public fascination with Bundy's case illustrates how women and sexual minorities still struggle to be seen as credible within broader society and the criminal justice system, and it also reveals that violence against women is fodder for entertainment. These cases serve as an entry point for forensic analysis (Chapter 3) and moral reflection (Chapter 4) on sexual violence and rape culture. Chapter 3 takes a deep dive into how criminality, gender, and justice inform investigators and the public's response to sexual violence. Why are most sexual crimes not prosecuted? What crimes are most likely to be given attention and why? How is the evidence gathered and where does it go? What laws and regulations govern this process? Chapter 4 concludes with a discussion of the ways in which white innocence and white entitlement participate in theological narratives of victim blaming and shaming within the context of sexual harassment and sexual violence.

The final three chapters unpack the role of true crime media in normalizing criminal and racial injustice. Chapter 5 places the case of the Central Park jogger—which ended with the wrongful convictions of Yusef Salaam, Korey Wise, Kevin Richardson, Raymond Santana, and Antron McCray, who came to be known as the Central Park Five—in conversation with the lived experiences of returning citizens. DNA testing played an important role in acquitting the men, but the case had a lasting impact on the daily lives of those wrongfully convicted and their families. We explore tactics that contemporary crime media employs to normalize injustice on the screen and to render racism invisible. In many instances the carceral system is presented as race neutral, thereby erasing its explicit connection to chattel slavery and Jim Crow–era segregation. Particular attention is given to narratives of resistance and to the challenges of reentry. Criminal sentences even for minor misdemeanors can have a lifelong impact on those convicted, restricting access to employment, housing, and many other aspects of society. While white liberals advocate for racial justice in the wake of national incidents, it is imperative to make the same commitment to dismantle white supremacy in our daily lives.

Chapter 6 examines how turning a blind eye to bias, particularly in forensic science, can contribute to criminal injustice. The paradoxical role of forensic science in wrongful convictions—it can both contribute to and resolve such convictions—highlights the need to examine and mitigate bias within the field. Forensic science cannot claim infallibility. Detailing potential sources of bias along with techniques to reduce their potential effects provides a framework that can be applied beyond the forensic science domain. The way the human brain works makes all individuals susceptible to bias, in both its conscious and unconscious forms, thereby requiring further understanding and self-examination.

The book considers the figure of the "Karen"[35] in chapter 7. While the figure of the "Karen" isn't always a white woman who calls the cops on a Black man in Central Park, she does pose serious questions about the insidious nature of white entitlement, white allegiances, and white desires to maintain moral goodness at all costs. What would a moral response for "Karens" and other "good white liberals" look like? White people must find a way to retell the stories of their lives that move away from the need to preserve white moral goodness at the expense of African American and Latino/a people. White people cannot be so concerned about their own salvation (goodness) that they fail to hear the stories of those around them. Instead, white Christians must "re-story" their lives by learning how to live life without absolution. This work begins at home.

---

[35] This term has come to refer pejoratively to a middle-aged white woman who comes across as entitled and demanding, as in the case of the white woman who called the police on a Black man in Central Park in May 2020, claiming without evidence that he was harassing her. See Henry Goldblatt, "A Brief History of 'Karen,'" *New York Times* (July 31, 2020).

1

TRUE CRIME AND CHRISTIAN ETHICS

The meaning of crime has been negotiated in the public sphere for centuries. Today, "true crime" is part of the U.S. entertainment sector, and its viewers are consumers. True crime sells itself as true. Yet, how often is the *true* in true crime critically evaluated or questioned? Moreover, how did it come to be?

A BRIEF HISTORY OF TRUE CRIME

This book uses the term *true crime* to refer to the narration of real crimes across mainstream media outlets such as books, films, television shows, and podcasts.[1] Most scholars locate the origins of modern true crime in the mid-twentieth century, as this period marks a distinctively new way of writing about crime, one that was "more sensitive to context, more psychologically

---

[1] This definition is adapted from Jean Murley's definition of true crime as a murder narrative in *The Rise of True Crime: 20th Century Murder and American Popular Culture* (Westport, CT: Praeger, 2008), 6. It is worth noting that there is little scholarly consensus on the term. For a review of the literature on this point, see Tanya Horeck, *Justice on Demand: True Crime in the Digital Streaming Era* (Detroit: Wayne State University Press, 2019), Kindle edition, 7–11.

sophisticated, more willing to make conjectures about the unknown thoughts and motives of killers."[2] Before this period, the
narration of murder focused on the spiritual condition of the
person committing the crime. In the seventeenth and eighteenth
centuries, stories of murder were circulated in society through
execution sermons, which were published in inexpensive pam-
phlets or broadsides. The minister would spend weeks or months
with the convicted person in order to elicit a confession, garner-
ing the necessary details to construct the sermon.[3] In the early
American Puritan community, murder was considered to be only
"one of many equally reprehensible sins."[4] A confession of sin
allowed community to execute the individual with the knowledge that their soul would restored before God, reestablishing
moral order within community.[5] In so doing, execution sermons
acted as a vivid reminder to the congregation of the dangers
of falling further into sin, and often prompted further confession and repentance among those in the pews. The tenor and
emphasis changed, however, when a Black person was executed.
In this context execution sermons conveyed the message that
the Black search for freedom deserves punishment.[6] Execution
sermons for Black people often included admonitions about
pleasing God through servile obedience to one's superior, thus
reinforcing the theological message that the order and morality
of society was linked to control of Black bodies.[7] As we discuss

---

[2] Murley, *The Rise of True Crime,* 2.

[3] Ibid., 7.

[4] Jean Murley, "Ordinary Sinners and Moral Aliens: The Murder Narratives
of Charles Brockden Brown and Edgar Allan Poe," in *Understanding Evil: An
Interdisciplinary Approach,* ed. Margaret Breen (Leiden: Brill Academic, 2003),
182.

[5] Ibid.

[6] Christophe D. Ringer, *Necropolitics: The Religious Crisis of Mass Incarceration*
(Lanham, MD: Lexington Books, 2021), 21.

[7] Ibid., 24.

throughout this book, these theological tropes continue in true crime media today.

Through the late 1800s and early 1900s, narratives changed as people became preoccupied with the biographical details of those who committed homicide. Language also became more ornate, and "horror-inflected rhetoric took over."[8] Readers not only wanted to know who the person was but also the gruesome details of what happened. Enlightenment emphases on rationality and social stability also coincided with a shift in the narration of murder and violent crime in the nineteenth century.[9] Those convicted of murder were no longer ordinary sinners; they were now "described as hideously outside the moral boundaries of humanity."[10] Accounts of crime were sensationalized, stressing the "moral monstrosity" of the act and the person who committed the crime.[11] By the end of the nineteenth century, developments in forensic science and psychology made it possible to provide an intimate description of what happened at a crime scene without actually being there. Journalists gathered information about crimes directly from the police. The narration of murder shifted again, from the sensational to a more objective tone with less melodramatic rhetoric, often including the textual recreation of crime as well as a scientific explanation of the evidence. This, when paired with twenty-first-century expectations regarding

---

[8] Murley, *The Rise of True Crime*, 8.

[9] In 1833, public demand for more details about crime gave rise to what was once called the penny press. The *New York Sun* and *The New York Herald*, among the first to publish daily crime news, were "known to publish sensationalized and fabricated information" in order to increase readership. Venessa Garcia, "News Media, Police in," in *The Social History of Crime and Punishment in America: An Encyclopedia*, ed. Wilbur Miller (Los Angeles: Sage, 2012), 1248–54. Also see Sidney I. Pomerantz, "The Press of a Greater New York, 1898–1900," *New York History* 39, no. 1 (1958): 58.

[10] Murley, *The Rise of True Crime,* 8.

[11] Ibid.

participatory media culture, has led to what we see today.[12] As we discuss in the chapters to come, aspects of true crime's etiology continue to include interest in biographical details, gruesome accounts of violence, and depictions of those who are convicted as moral monsters.

TRUE CRIME AS TRUE?

True crime occupies a place in American public discourse where rhetoric about evil and the human condition are continually renegotiated. Rachel Monroe explains:

> The murder stories we tell, and the ways that we tell them, have a political and social impact and are worth taking seriously. Lessons are embedded within their gory details. When read closely, they can reveal the anxieties of the moment, tell us who's allowed to be a victim, and teach us what our monsters are supposed to look like.[13]

The narratives we create and absorb about crime and justice unearth community norms regarding interpretations of violence; they also demarcate the boundaries of inclusion and exclusion.

True crime focuses on storytelling by making the crimes exciting and entertaining to viewers—while often forgetting the humanity of the victims and survivors and the affected communities. This repackaging of the story separates violence from its social and scientific contexts. Framing tactics involving emotional identification with, and distancing from, the individual suspected of the crime are overlaid with elements of mystery and suspense. These tactics are often presented through the familiar

---

[12] Horeck, *Justice on Demand*, 6.

[13] Rachel Monroe, *Savage Appetites: Four True Stories of Women, Crime, and Obsession* (New York: Scribner, 2019), Kindle edition, 9.

tropes of voyeurism, seriality, voice-overs, and violent depictions of death.[14] Violence is presented as the result of hidden threats in a seemingly innocuous environment and is almost always spectacularly gruesome.

Television shows like *Law & Order: Special Victims Unit* present the criminal justice system very simplistically: (1) A person commits a crime, is arrested by the police, and goes to jail; (2) after posting bail, the person quickly faces trial by jury; and (3) if convicted, the person goes to prison. In reality, however, the carceral system is hardly straightforward. It is a labyrinth of laws, agencies, and courts. People can spend years in jail before seeing a judge, and plea deals, not jury trials, solve most cases.[15] Prisons are not exciting places to be, and life can be lonely, tedious, and boring. None of this is shown on television. Furthermore, shows like *CSI: Crime Scene Investigation* and other media that focus on forensic science skew public perceptions by dramatizing testing techniques and exaggerating the availability and quality of evidence in a given case.[16] Mainstream media further emphasize that these expectations can have a negative impact on real-life court outcomes because jurors place too much weight on scientific evidence or the lack thereof.[17] While forensic science plays a critical role in the courtroom, it has limitations. The public does

---

[14] Murley, *The Rise of True Crime*, 82–84. As used here, the term *seriality* has a dual referent: the serial killer, and the way in which true crime is streamed through the docuseries. One of the key attributes of true crime media is that it is conducive to binge watching or streaming in the sense that a show ends with a "hook," something that drives the viewer to tune in to the next episode.

[15] Monroe, *Savage Appetites,* 9.

[16] N. J. Schweitzer and Michael J. Saks, "The CSI Effect: Popular Fiction about Forensic Science Affects the Public's Expectations about Real Forensic Science," *Jurimetrics* (2007): 357–64.

[17] Research has proven that shows like *CSI* increase expectations related to forensic science evidence, but no studies have definitively proven an impact on trial outcomes. Simon A. Cole and Rachel Dioso-Villa, "Investigating the 'CSI Effect' Effect: Media and Litigation Crisis in Criminal Law," *Stanford Law Review* 61, no. 6 (2009): 1335–73.

not generally understand this due to false media representations. Public perceptions play a critical role in the administration of justice, and the "*CSI* Effect," which refers to unrealistic expectations that jurors have regarding scientific evidence presented in courts, can potentially be a detriment to the jurors' evaluation of evidence, resulting in an unjust outcome (such as a wrongful conviction or a wrongful acquittal).[18]

Of particular importance for this book is the role of true crime media in shaping how people interpret justice, innocence, and guilt. Studies have repeatedly shown that the majority of people in the United States name the media as their primary source of information (if not the only source) about the criminal justice system. Crime media plays a powerful role in the absence of substantial life experience with the criminal justice system.[19] While most people recognize that crime and justice media are "unrealistic and heavily edited," researchers have found that "continued exposure to the content influences one's view of reality, and this influence increases in areas where alternate sources

---

[18] Steven M. Smith, Veronica Stinson, and Marc W. Patry, "Fact or Fiction: The Myth and Reality of the CSI Effect," *Court Review* 47, no. 1–2 (2011): 4–7. A 2006 research study examining the "CSI effect" confirmed enhanced juror expectations and hypothesized a larger "tech effect." Beyond shows like *CSI,* advancements in technology and information distribution within popular culture inform juror expectations and demands, requiring the criminal justice system to adapt to these changes. See Donald E. Shelton, Young S. Kim, and Gregg Barak, "A Study of Juror Expectations and Demands concerning Scientific Evidence: Does the CSI Effect Exist?" *Vanderbilt Journal of Entertainment and Technology Law* 9, no. 2 (2006): 331–68.

[19] The relationship between media viewing and direct personal experience with the criminal justice system is a complex and emerging field of research. For more, see Lisa Kort-Butler and Patrick Habecker, "Framing and Cultivating the Story of Crime: The Effects of Media Use, Victimization, and Social Networks on Attitudes about Crime," *Criminal Justice Review* 43, no. 2 (2018): 127–46.

of information are less available."[20] This holds increased relevance in a digital era, as 85 percent of Americans report going online daily, with 31 percent reporting that they are online constantly.[21] And according to recent data from the Pew Research Center, approximately half of people under fifty say they are online constantly, thus making critical reflection on crime and justice in the media a crucial task for all generations. At stake is not only the normalization of violence but the blurring of fact and fiction through looping techniques and inaccurate representation of science. For example, the tagline of the podcast *Murder Minute* reads: "This is not for the faint of heart. Murder Minute stories are detailed and with photos and videos of crime scenes and serial killers. All of our stories are thoroughly researched and 100% true. Our writers are respectful of the victims and do not glorify or condone violence but be warned that some of these stories are very disturbing."[22] Many true-crime consumers believe, or at a minimum cannot discern, whether what is represented on the screen reflects a fair and honest representation of circumstances.[23]

While the stories recounted in true crime media are about actual events, they are always "shaped by the teller and his or her values and beliefs about such events";[24] it follows that there are often many different stories and interpretations of the same

---

[20] Ray Surette, *Media, Crime, and Criminal Justice: Images, Realities, and Policies*, 5th edition (Stamford, CT: Cengage Learning, 2014), 4. Also see Kort-Butler and Habecker, "Framing and Cultivating the Story of Crime."

[21] See Andrew Perrin and Sara Atske, "About Three-in-Ten US Adults Say They Are 'Almost Constantly' Online," *Pew Research Center*, March 26.

[22] *Murder Minute—True Crime*, podcast, Banter App.

[23] Murley, *True Crime*, 13. Also see Venessa Garcia and Samantha Arkerson, *Crime, Media, and Reality: Examining Mixed Messages about Crime and Justice in Popular Media* (Lanham, MD: Rowman & Littlefield: 2018), chaps. 1 and 7; Garcia and Arkerson offer a thorough discussion and review of the social construction of crime and justice in different media outlets.

[24] Murley, *True Crime*, 6.

events. As cultural historian Karen Halttunen elaborates, "Any story of murder involves a fictive process, which reveals much about the mental and emotional strategies employed within a given historical culture for responding to serious transgression in its midst."[25] In this way, the American construction of true crime digital media participates in and responds to the cultural norms of the society in which it is created. Current trends in true crime media reveal a worldview that is "suspicious and cynical, narrowly focused on the worst kinds of crimes, and preoccupied with safety, order, and justice."[26] The shows contain videos and photos of autopsies, gunshot wounds, bruises, and close-ups of bloodstains, paired with extensive biographical information about the individual under investigation.

While there is quite a bit of variety within the true crime genre, most shows rely upon a standard formula that includes a combination of reenactment, contextualization, and detection to capture the attention of the audience.[27] For example, documentary reenactments rely heavily on visual production techniques to build suspense, often only revealing the details of the crime at the end of the show. Two examples that we discuss in this book are Ava DuVernay's *When They See Us* and Joe Berlinger's *Extremely Wicked, Shockingly Evil and Vile.*

While true crime media can be very entertaining, it's important to realize that it also plays a critical role in shaping how the public understands justice and safety. Everyone wants to feel *safe* and many Christians value *justice,* but it is imperative to ask critical questions about the meaning and construction of these terms. Justice for whom? Safety for whom? As we will

---

[25] Karen Halttunen, *Murder Most Foul: The Killer and the American Gothic Imagination* (Cambridge, MA: Harvard University Press, 2000), 2.

[26] Ibid.

[27] Murley, *The Rise of True Crime*, 127. Exceptions to this are news programs like *48 Hours Mystery*, which do not use reenactments due to journalistic standards.

discuss, true crime sets forth a vision of justice that reinforces
and reifies existing social structures and public policies within
the criminal justice system, most of which systemically disadvantage and oppress African American and Latino/a people.[28]
Throughout history, white interests have informed definitions
of safety and justice, even in more mundane spaces.[29] In this
way, true crime media protects the interests of privileged
people through its expression of violence and justice. This will
be especially evident when we take a closer look at systemic
inequalities, such as sexual and racialized forms of violence, in
Chapters 2 and 5.

The worldview produced by true crime media is a white
worldview. At true crime conventions, fans can be seen sporting
t-shirts that read "BASICALLY A DETECTIVE" and "DNA
OR IT DIDN'T HAPPEN" and "I'M JUST HERE TO ES-
TABLISH AN ALIBI."[30] The sayings on these shirts not only
reveal unrealistic expectations about the efficaciousness of the
criminal justice system and the tools of forensic science, but
also points to moral indifference to radical inequities rampant
within the criminal justice system itself. For example, as we
unpack throughout this book, gathering and analyzing DNA is
a lengthy and complex process and may not provide definitive
grounds for guilt or innocence in a particular case. Even more
problematic is the way that true crime claims to be "true" and
rooted in scientific objectivity. On television, audiences are intro-
duced to complex scientific terminology and legal terminology
such as *mens rea,* blood spatter, DNA analysis, and so on. They
are even shown snippets of evidence from actual cases. However,
it's important to note that irrespective of its capacity to provide

---

[28] For a detailed analysis see Michelle Alexander, *The New Jim Crow: Mass Incarceration in the Age of Colorblindness* (New York: New Press, 2010).

[29] Robin DiAngelo, *White Fragility: Why It's So Hard for White People to Talk about Race* (Boston: Beacon Press, 2018), 126–27.

[30] Monroe, *Savage Appetites,* 2.

conclusive evidence for a specific case, the discipline of forensic science, on its own, is unable to address patterns of systemic injustices such as the cultural acceptance of violence against women, racial profiling and policing, or economic inequality. Moral analysis is needed to tackle these broader issues.

The entertainment factor of true crime media implies that the criminal justice system can be reduced to a game where participants are positioned as amateur detectives, given bits and pieces of evidence, and encouraged to debate innocence or guilt.[31] In this game, winning is equated with scientific certainty (solving a case) and a conviction. From the standpoint of moral theology, this is a rather dangerous game to play because it encourages voyeurism and passive bystanding in the face of radical human suffering. This is of particular significance given racial disparities within the United States criminal justice system.

The United States incarcerates the greatest number of people per capita in the world.[32] This is not because we have the highest crime rate, however. Beginning in the 1980s, sentencing policies related to the "War on Drugs" spurred increased incarceration rates.[33] The population of individuals serving life sentences has almost quintupled since the 1980s despite a decrease in violent crimes for the past twenty years.[34] Racial disparities in incarceration rates reveal that the imprisonment rate for Black men is 5.7 times the rate for white men,[35] and these disparities cannot

---

[31] Tanya Horeck makes this point in relation to the podcast *Serial* in *Justice on Demand*, 135–36. I (Elisabeth) believe it can be applied in a much broader context.

[32] Roy Walmsley, "World Prison Population List, Twelfth Edition," *World Prison Brief: Institute for Criminal Policy Research* (2018).

[33] Alexander, *The New Jim Crow*, 89–93, 112–14. For example, in *Hutto v. Davis* (1982) the US Supreme Court upholds forty years of imprisonment for an attempt to sell nine ounces of marijuana.

[34] "Criminal Justice Facts," *The Sentencing Project*, 2020.

[35] E. Ann Carson, "Prisoners in 2019," Bureau of Justice Statistics, October 2020.

be explained by corresponding differences in offending rates.[36] Studies indicate that higher percentages of Black and Latino men are incarcerated because of (1) policies and practices that disadvantage minorities (e.g., cash bail); (2) implicit bias and stereotypes (e.g., by judges, police, etc.); and (3) "structural disadvantages in communities of color which are associated with high rates of offending and arrest."[37] As moral theologian Amy Levad points out, mass incarceration not only has a lasting effect on the individuals incarcerated and their families, but it also impacts the "well-being of entire communities."[38] Mr. L., a member of the Elsinore-Bennu Think Tank for Restorative Justice, describes the collateral effects of incarceration as removing an entire generation of grandfathers from the community. Incarceration has taken away the opportunity to pass down practical wisdom, to share stories, and mentor the next generation. True crime media does not tell this story. True crime media also does not tell the story of how privileged people benefit from the present-day policies and procedures (e.g., cheap labor). The problem is that most people do not even know what they are missing.

WHY TRUE CRIME AND CHRISTIAN ETHICS?

At present, very little has been published that explores the Western phenomena of true crime and its impact on the Western Christian moral imagination. This is surprising given significant developments within the past several decades in Christian theology and ethics in three areas: criminal justice, popular culture and media, and science. However, there have been a number of

---

[36] Alfred Blumstein, "Racial Disproportionality of US Prison Populations Revisited," *University of Colorado Law Review* 64, no. 3 (1993): 743–60.

[37] Ashley Nellis, "The Color of Justice: Racial and Ethnic Disparity in State Prisons," *The Sentencing Project* (June 14, 2016), 9.

[38] Amy Levad, *Redeeming a Prison Society: A Liturgical and Sacramental Response to Mass Incarceration* (Minneapolis: Fortress Press, 2014), 37.

scholars within Christian theology and ethics who have taken a critical look at mass incarceration, including Kelly Brown Douglas, Joshua Dubler, Katherine Getek Soltis, Amy Levad, Vincent Lloyd, Nikia Smith Robert, and Mark Lewis Taylor.[39] Their work lays the foundation for this book.

While many scholars mention true crime media, there has yet to be an interdisciplinary and intersectional systematic moral reflection on the significance of true crime media in shaping the Christian moral imagination concerning anti-Blackness and violence against women, two issues we emphasize in this book.[40] We believe this is an essential topic for Christian ethics because most people, predominantly white privileged people, encounter crime through a screen (television, movie, computer, etc.). In this way, we are bystanders and witnesses to violence. While scholars increasingly engage popular culture and media studies, few theological resources integrate media literacy, media studies, and moral reflection on sexual violence and anti-Blackness, although scholars like Miguel De La Torre, Elías Ortega-Aponte, and

---

[39] These are just a few examples of many. See Kelly Brown Douglas, *Stand Your Ground: Black Bodies and the Justice of God* (Maryknoll, NY: Orbis Books, 2015); Mark Lewis Taylor, *The Executed God: The Way of the Cross in Lockdown America* (Minneapolis: Fortress Press, 2007); Levad, *Redeeming a Prison Society*; Katherine Getek Soltis, "Mass Incarceration and Theological Images of Justice," *Journal of the Society of Christian Ethics* 31, no. 2 (2011): 113–30; James H. Cone, *The Cross and the Lynching Tree* (Maryknoll, NY: Orbis Books, 2013); Joshua Dubler and Vincent Lloyd, *Break Every Yoke: Religion, Justice, and the Abolition of Prisons* (New York: Oxford, 2019); and Nikia Smith Robert, "Penitence, Plantation and the Penitentiary: A Liberation Theology for Lockdown America," *The Graduate Journal of Harvard Divinity School* 12 (2017): 41–69.

[40] Many scholars have examined popular media and religion, such as M. Jess Peacock, *Such a Dark Thing: Theology of the Vampire Narrative in Popular Culture* (Eugene, OR: Wipf & Stock, 2015); Clive Marsh, *A Cultural Theology of Salvation* (New York: Oxford, 2018); and Megan Goodwin, *Abusing Religion: Literary Persecution, Sex Scandals, and American Minority Religions* (New Brunswick, NJ: Rutgers University Press, 2018). But while these manuscripts offer essential resources, many of them are narrow in scope and few cross over explicitly into Christian ethics.

Eboni Marshall Turman have begun the conversation in significant ways.[41] Yet, little work has been done to integrate forensic science and Christian ethics. Forensic science and criminology have given considerable attention to true crime media. Yet, these fields do not always ask the moral questions necessary for bringing about systemic change.[42]

While theology and science diverge substantively in methodological approaches, the stark juxtaposition between faith and science within the popular sphere is a false one that can detract from more significant issues at stake for society: justice and equity. When it comes to science and tech issues, Christian theologians and ethicists struggle to ask the right kinds of questions. In part, this is because the method of study does not always reflect how ordinary people engage with the subject matter in lived time and space. Across the country, humanities and tech research are separated by discipline. Yet, science, ethics, and technology are not static fragmented entities that a user engages now and then; they are integrated into a fluid, ever-changing interface. The emergence of TikTok is a case in point—most of

---

[41] Examples include Miguel De La Torre's work in constructing the *Trails of Hope and Terror*, directed by Vincent De La Torre (Centennial, CO: V1 Educational Media, 2016). Also see Elías Ortega-Aponte, "The Haunting of the Lynching Spectacles," in *Anti-Blackness and Christian Ethics*, ed. Vincent W. Lloyd and Andrew Prevot (Maryknoll, NY: Orbis Books, 2017), 111–30; and Ringer, *Necropolitics*.

[42] While many texts focus on the forensic science evidence associated with criminal cases, few focus on its role in popular culture. The textbook *Illusion of Justice: Inside Making a Murderer and America's Broken System* (New York: Harper, 2017), by Jerome F. Buting, examines the Steven Avery case depicted in the Netflix series *Making a Murderer*. In this text the role of forensic science in relation to wrongful convictions is examined through the eyes of a criminal defense lawyer. Other texts that look at wrongful convictions and the role of forensic science include Brent E. Turvey and Craig M. Cooley, *Miscarriages of Justice: Actual Innocence, Forensic Evidence, and the Law* (New York: Academic Press, 2014); and Mark Godsey, *Blind Injustice: A Former Prosecutor Exposes the Psychology and Politics of Wrongful Convictions* (Oakland, CA: University of California Press, 2017).

our students are on the platform because it is entertaining and because this is how they connect with their peers; they want to be part of the cultural phenomenon. But when users upload videos or follow other users on TikTok, they are not always aware of what personal information they are giving away and/ or who can see it. Algorithms generate suggestions of who to follow based upon the content you post, your usage, geographical location, profile, and so forth. Yet, this data, which is also sold to marketing firms, can be used to identify locations or activity in a missing person's case. The average user rarely stops to reflect upon the moral implications of their participation on TikTok; we swipe, tap, and click.[43] Therefore, re-imagining the way in which we do theology and ethics is in and of itself a critical and necessary moral task.

As we will discuss, the representation of crime in true crime operates semi-independently of crime itself. This is irrespective of the intention of the author of the book or film producer. This means that the depiction of a crime (such as a rape, homicide, or assault) in true crime is not identical to what actually happened; nor will it adhere exactly to the viewer's cultural understanding of rape, homicide, or assault. This is because those who tell the story and listen to the story are socially situated, as we discuss below.

CHRISTIAN ETHICS AS A
PROCESS OF MORAL GROWTH

Throughout Western Christian history, many have assumed that the best pathway to knowing is through rational, logical, and autonomous thinking. In the Enlightenment, reason reigned supreme. For René Descartes (1596–1650), the aim of philosophy

---

[43] To date, no one has engaged in a sustained interdisciplinary analysis of true crime within the field of Christian ethics.

was to seek out abstract universal principles that could form the foundation for knowledge itself—that is, how do I know what I know? In his search for certainty, Descartes attempts to remove everything that might distract from his search for knowledge of the subject at hand, including bodily concerns, people, or ethical commitments. Descartes famously concludes: "I think, therefore, I am." The biggest challenge with Descartes's paradigm is not the presupposition itself but rather the assumptions embedded within. For Descartes, Truth (with a capital T) is objective and universal. Inherent in this is the assumption that it is possible to "abstract oneself from our cultural and social location and to see with unbiased eyes."[44] If true, this would mean that a person's social situatedness (such as their race, sexual identity, religious background, and cultural and geographical location) would have no bearing on their interpretation of reality. Descartes also assumes that the body and mind can be separated and that emotion and embodied knowledge are of little consequence; he valued only highly rationalized, independent calculation. In the United States, we still use these defaults when considering who counts as smart, capable, or intelligent. For example, white males still account for almost 90 percent of the CEOs in Fortune 500 companies.[45]

The criteria of autonomy, rationality, and individuality were also considered to be preeminent markers in moral decision-making in the Western Christian tradition. Anglo-educated clergymen were considered to be the most well-equipped to provide moral guidance at the personal and individual level. Moral manuals stressed a legal model of morality in which moral behavior

---

[44] Schneider and Ray, *Awake to the Moment*, 43. Also see René Descartes, *Discourse on Method*, trans. John Veitch, Project Gutenberg, esp. part IV.

[45] Richie Zweigenhaft, "Fortune 500 CEOs, 2000–2020: Still Male, Still White," *The Society Pages*, October 28, 2020.

was equated with obedience to God's law.[46] While most Catholic
moral theologians no longer espouse a rigid legalistic approach
to morality, it still lingers within the public sphere.[47] That is, too
often, people think of moral reasoning as a once-and-for-all,
static process, wherein an external authority tells us what to do,
when to do it, and how to do it. A legalistic approach to moral
decision-making might be helpful in limited contexts for holding
particular persons responsible, but it is incapable of addressing
the privileged complicity in structural violence like white racism because of the insidious nature of white racism itself. To use
Black Catholic moral theologian Bryan Massingale's terminology,
white racism is "culturally entrenched."[48] Within such a legalistic
framework, morality often dissolves into a laundry list of "dos"
and "don'ts" regarding specific actions. Moreover, not only has
the obsession with defining "right" and "wrong" behavior historically been used to denigrate those on the margins, but, in this
case, such language has been appropriated to evoke a rhetoric
of guilt and shame. For example, within the context of intimate
violence, guilt and shame create lasting wounds and have prevented many survivors from getting the help they need. We also
have to ask critical questions about who is defining what counts
as "good" and "bad" behavior in the first place. This is important
because of the dynamics of power within theological discourse
itself. While progress is being made, the majority of people who
write about theology and train theologians at universities are still
white. Their questions and concerns have shaped the landscape
of the discipline for centuries. For example, when considering
the relationship of science and religion, many white scholars

---

[46] See Charles Curran, *The Development of Moral Theology: Five Strands*
(Washington, DC: Georgetown University Press, 2013), 14–22.

[47] Kate Ott, *Christian Ethics for a Digital Society* (Lanham, MD: Rowman &
Littlefield, 2019), 4.

[48] Bryan N. Massingale, *Racial Justice and the Catholic Church* (Maryknoll,
NY: Orbis Books, 2010), 25.

begin with the relationship between creation and evolution.[49] Yet, this question is not relevant to those who are suffering the trauma of racist insults and injuries, often on a daily basis. It is a white question.[50]

It is crucial to understand that "whiteness" is ingrained within white subjectivity. This makes it difficult for white people to recognize accurately what Black theologian James Cone has named the sin of whiteness.[51] As Cone explains, "Sin is a community concept. . . . There can be no knowledge of the sinful condition except in the movement of an oppressed community claiming its freedom. This means that whites, despite their self-proclaimed righteousness, are rendered incapable of making valid judgments on the character of sin. . . . In white theology, sin is a theoretical idea, not a concrete reality."[52] Cone's statement highlights how white racial privilege supports the tacit acceptance of violence through the luxury of obliviousness. Whiteness is about power and entitlement.[53] Whiteness grants those in positions of power the ability to decide whom to tolerate, whom to ignore, and whom to help. White privilege distorts white people's view of reality. It tricks white people into believing it is appropriate to make moral claims, by themselves, for everyone else. This is strange because white people are not Black, Latino/a, Asian, or

---

[49] Philip Clayton reviewed the literature to see what had been published in *Zygon* in the past sixty years and noted that the starting point of creation/evolution remained a central question for many decades in the conversation between science and religion. Not once is race mentioned. See "The Fruits of Pluralism: A Vision for the Next Seven Years in Religion/Science," *Zygon: The Journal of Religion and Science* 49, no. 2 (2014): 430–42.

[50] Miguel De La Torre makes this point in *Reading the Bible from the Margins* (Maryknoll, NY: Orbis Books, 2013), 48.

[51] James H. Cone, *A Black Theology of Liberation*, 40th anniv. ed. (Maryknoll, NY: Orbis Books, 2010), 115.

[52] Ibid., 113.

[53] W. E. B. Du Bois, "The Souls of White Folk," in *Charleston Syllabus: Readings on Race, Racism, and Racial Violence*, ed. Chad Williams, Kidada E. Williams, and Kiesha N. Blain (Athens: The University of Georgia Press, 2016): 177–81.

Indigenous. In fact, on the whole, white people do not know very much about the lived realities of people of color. The majority of white people live in white neighborhoods and hang out with white friends. White Christians go to white churches. Even for those who are aware of their own complicity in the dynamics of white racism and who make active attempts toward racial justice, awareness is not as straightforward as we would like to think.

As critical race philosopher George Yancy explains, "To be white in America is always already to be implicated in power."[54] Whiteness is constantly being embedded within white subjectivity itself, and thus, white self-reflection on race, racism, and white privilege requires a special kind of vigilance. In order to facilitate this process, the sense of self-certainty rooted in white people's view of the world must be debunked. It is precisely in those moments when I'm sure I'm right that I most need to "look and listen and check and question."[55] A legalistic moral framework fails to account adequately for the dynamic nature of power relationships within society; a less rigid, more nuanced approach is needed to identify and dismantle unjust societal frameworks.

In *Christian Ethics for a Digital Society*, Kate Ott suggests that ethics is a process of moral growth that "requires a sensibility to more than a set of rules."[56] Ott likens moral decision-making to an art. While moral guidelines and ethical principles have their place, we cannot restrict our ethical thinking to them. This is because moral decision-making is about finding "better solutions, not one right answer."[57] We also need to ask better moral

---

[54] George Yancy, *Black Bodies, White Gazes: The Continuing Significance of Race* (Lanham, MD: Rowman & Littlefield, 2008), 235.

[55] Marilyn Frye, *The Politics of Reality: Essays in Feminist Theory* (Freedom, CA: Crossing, 1983), 75.

[56] Ott, *Christian Ethics for a Digital Society*, 5.

[57] Ibid., 6.

questions. Moral approaches must translate to everyday living. In order to do this, one has to understand how systems work. Ott describes this as "developing a socially minded curiosity that often starts with observations about how personal experience connects to larger social patterns."[58] Media literacy is a form of conscientization, or critical consciousness, rooted in reflection and action upon sociohistorical reality.[59] Drawing upon the work of Paulo Freire, Ott suggests that the praxis of conscientization must be developed in community and attentive to power dynamics. Ott's understanding of ethics as a process of creative moral response is helpful for this project, given its interdisciplinary scope and the fluid nature of forensic science and true crime media.

Forensic science is a field rooted in the complex interplay of objectivity and ongoing discovery. In basic terms, forensic science is the application of science to matters related to the legal system. Forensic scientists are members of the criminal justice system charged with upholding justice through science. There are numerous forensic science disciplines, each of which provides essential information by analyzing evidence. The most commonly examined type of evidence is associative, which can be used to associate or dissociate an individual to or from a crime. This kind of evidence includes hairs, fibers, body fluids, paint, bullets, and fingerprints.[60] However, the field is constantly developing due to the advent of new technologies. The increased sensitivity of DNA testing and advanced searching techniques have raised serious questions about the ethics of privacy. For example, DNA testing examines evidence to find the presence

---

[58] Ibid., 7.

[59] Ott makes this point. See Paulo Freire, "Cultural Action and Conscientization," *Harvard Educational Review* 68, no. 4 (1998): 499–521.

[60] Stuart H. James, Jon J. Nordby, and Suzanne Bell, *Forensic Science: An Introduction to Scientific and Investigative Techniques*, 4th ed. (Boca Raton, FL: CRC Press/Taylor & Francis Group, 2014), 28–35.

of biological material with the goal of determining whose DNA it is. Traditionally, direct comparisons have been performed between evidence and a known reference. With advanced searching techniques, it is now possible to search for relatives who partially match the evidence DNA by using ancestry databases in order to find the individual who is connected to the DNA evidence. The 2018 identification of the Golden State Killer, Joseph DeAngelo, used investigative genetic genealogy techniques, and the ancestry DNA database search sparked further privacy concern debates.[61] While the technology exists to perform advanced DNA testing and searching, the application of such techniques raises moral concerns about individual privacy rights versus public safety. Similarly, popular culture is an ever-changing entity. For example, new social media apps are emerging constantly, from the aforementioned TikTok to Clubhouse. For this reason, media literacy, as a moral praxis within an interdisciplinary context, requires moral formation within the context of a local community.

Who we are, who we hope to be, and what we believe is important is shaped by those who are most proximate. In part, this is why taking account of geography (or location) matters greatly when it comes to ethics and moral formation. The people who have the greatest influence on our moral formation are our friends and families, and those with whom we go to school and socialize. This has natural consequences. It really does matter with whom you spend your time. For example, white people who live in predominantly white communities are necessarily shaped by whiteness. At the same time, as human beings we are endowed with agency. We are constantly learning new things. The human spirit is not intractable; it is ever changing. That is a beautiful thing because it means you have the power to make a difference

---

[61] Megan Molteni, "What the Golden State Killer Tells Us about Forensic Genetics," *Wired*, April 24, 2019.

in the lives of other people. What you do matters. The ways that you educate your children matter. Therefore, the work of media literacy must begin at home, in schools, in parishes, and in your neighborhood. This book aims to help address that need. We hope that you will join us on the journey.

2

DEAD BODIES, SEXUAL VIOLENCE, AND TRUE CRIME

As a student, Alex was articulate, bright, and funny. Several weeks into the semester, however, she stopped coming to my class. After she failed the midterm exam, I (Elisabeth) invited her to my office. Alex shared that she had recently broken up with her partner and was having a hard time keeping up with schoolwork. The relationship had been wonderful at first. In public, it was a fairytale romance, but in private, it became a completely different story. Alex's partner was jealous, possessive, and constantly accused her of cheating. She also felt pressured to engage in sexual acts that she wasn't quite sure she wanted to do. The breaking point came when Alex had a group project in her biology class. Her partner threatened to break up with her if she went to the group meeting, which was at another student's house. Alex complied and failed the assignment. As we processed what had happened and what still was to come, Alex kept saying to me: "How could I have been so stupid? How could I let this happen to me? I am so embarrassed." It was a lot of shame to carry.[1]

---

[1] Names and details have been altered to protect the identity of those involved.

While sexual violence can take many forms, irrespective of the circumstances, healing from it is very hard. Despite our best intentions, as communities, we continue to miss this point. Dr. Christine Blasey Ford's testimony regarding allegations of sexual assault at a Senate hearing in Brett Kavanaugh's nomination for the US Supreme Court was interpreted along political party lines, and then absorbed into our nation's partisan divide.[2] It seemed that what mattered most to the American public was what side you were on, and who won. Many people lost sight of the fact that sexual violence may have occurred at all.[3] Reflecting on the situation, I wrote:

> What Dr. Ford is doing is both ordinary and extraordinary. Survivors do this every day in a culture that eroticizes violence against women and people of color, as the trauma of sexual violence is carried in the body, the soul, and the mind. What people don't realize is how hard the healing is. The healing wouldn't be half as hard without the name-calling, the threats to silence, the constant questioning of credibility, and the fracturing of community.
>
> Yet, these things exist even apart from hearings and testimonies. They are the very foundation upon which sexual violence is normalized. This is what makes her testimony ordinary.
>
> You see, the bigger question isn't who remembered what facts, or who is lying. It isn't whose side you are on, or what team is winning. Sexual violence isn't a game in which there are winners and losers. Rather, in a world in which relationship violence exists, everyone loses. The real

---

[2] For example, see "How Americans across the Country Are Reacting to Christine Blasey Ford's Testimony," *New York Times,* September 27, 2018.

[3] From a judicial standpoint, this case involved allegations of sexual assault. I (Elisabeth) believe sexual assault occurred.

question is, how can we keep letting this happen in our communities?

SEXUAL VIOLENCE AND MEDIA REPRESENTATION

American media outlets present a partial picture of sexual violence, one that promotes and perpetuates rape culture. Media representations are informed by dominant social attitudes about sex, race, and gender, as well as by institutionalized racism and sexism within the media industry.[4] Today, voyeuristic stories about allegations of sexual violence against celebrities like Harvey Weinstein and Bill Cosby make for "good media copy"[5] and high television ratings. Yet, media coverage regularly overlooks and decontextualizes abuse, objectifies survivors, and privileges the presumption of white innocence.[6] In such a framework, survivors are responsible for "keeping themselves safe," for presenting forensic evidence to the police, and for convincing the public that they are trustworthy, reliable, and responsible citizens. As religious studies scholar Megan Goodwin argues, "This kind of literature presents female pain as both obscene and titillating, enthralling audiences with vivid accounts of white women violated by savage outsiders."[7] Such framing is not only misleading, as most incidents of sexual violence occur among known parties,

---

[4] Jenny Kitzinger, "Rape in the Media," in *Rape: Challenging Contemporary Thinking*, ed. Miranda A. H. Horvath and Jennifer M. Brown (New York: Routledge, 2009), 75.

[5] Ibid. Also see Rosemary Pennington and Jessica Birthisel, "When New Media Make News: Framing Technology and Sexual Assault in the Steubenville Rape Case," *New Media and Society* 18, no. 11 (2016): 2348.

[6] Kitzinger, "Rape in the Media," 76, 82.

[7] Megan Goodwin, *Abusing Religion: Literary Persecution, Sex Scandals, and American Minority Religions* (New Brunswick, NJ: Rutgers University Press, 2019), Kindle edition, 6.

but it also does little to resolve the issue because it obscures the role of the community. The root cause of the violation is misattributed to a "problematic relationship," "bad person," or "bad day."[8] For Christians, such narratives play out in verticalizing patterns of sin, whereby accountability for harm is predominantly worked out between God and the individual. As I have illustrated elsewhere, such a framework not only leaves us wanting in terms of theological language to describe the depths of the damage that is done by systemic evil and trauma, but it also fails to capture the ways in which unethical passivity, inaction, and silence are sinful.[9] In doing so, we are able to convince ourselves that the violation is not that bad or not our problem.

In the true crime serial, violence against women takes center stage.[10] As mentioned previously, women have long been acknowledged as the core audience for true crime. This phenomenon began in the 1970s and 1980s with the work of author Ann Rule and is built around the assumption that women need to be vigilant against men who are potentially violent.[11] Rule, a former Seattle police officer and friend of Ted Bundy, saw her writing as a way of providing young women with information on how to deal with potentially dangerous situations: "When I began writing fact-detective stories I promised myself I would remember I was writing about the loss of human beings. I hoped the work might somehow save other victims. I

---

[8] A recent example of this would be when a Georgia officer described a twenty-one-year-old white man's shooting spree at several spas in the Atlanta area as the result of a "really bad day." Rex Huppke, "Atlanta Shooting Suspect's 'Bad Day' and the Whitewashing of White Crime," *Chicago Tribune*, March 17, 2021.

[9] For a fuller discussion, see Elisabeth T. Vasko, *Beyond Apathy: A Theology for Bystanders* (Minneapolis: Fortress Press, 2015), 124–32.

[10] See Tanya Horeck, *Justice on Demand: True Crime in the Digital Streaming Era* (Detroit: Wayne State University Press, 2019), 128ff.

[11] Ann Rule is best known for her book *The Stranger beside Me* (New York: Simon & Schuster, 1980).

never wanted to seek out the sensational and the gory."[12] At the same time, Rule churned out dozens of fictional stories based upon case files.

While true crime audiences tend to be female, it has historically been men who tell the stories. Karen Kilgariff and Georgia Hardstack's podcast *My Favorite Murder* (MFM) breaks this tradition as it seeks to disrupt the cultures of toxic masculinity that surround rape culture. The podcast, in which Hardstack and Kilgariff recount real-life crimes and share their responses, is known for "wry humor and a focus on the overlooked (mostly female) victims of infamous (mostly male) killers."[13] The idea, according to Kilgariff, who coined the "murderino" fan culture's famous catch phrase "toxic masculinity ruins the party again," is that talking about murder will help ward off some of the anxieties women face about violence.[14] One of the central claims of MFM is that "women love to know all the terrible details of murder cases so that they can gain some sort of power over culturally endemic narratives in which girls and women are brutalized."[15] To be clear, Kilgariff and Hardstack are not laughing at homicide, rape, or abduction. Rather, "the humor comes from their irreverent, foul-mouthed banter as they share their personal responses to crimes."[16] As feminist media scholar Tanya Horeck suggests, MFM capitalizes upon and invites the listener's affective response and judgment. While MFM does change the dynamics of true crime storytelling, Horeck argues that the podcast itself does not

---

[12] Quoted in Victoria Beale, "Too Close to Ted Bundy," *New Yorker*, October 10, 2015.

[13] Alex Hawgood, "Grisly Murders and Serial Killers? Ooh, Tell Me More," *New York Times*, May 19, 2018.

[14] See Andrea DenHoed, "The *My Favorite Murder* Problem," *The New Republic*, November 22, 2019. Fans of MFM affectionately refer to themselves as murderinos.

[15] Horeck, *Justice on Demand,* 2. Hence the motto of the show: "Stay sexy and fuck politeness."

[16] Ibid.

challenge the dominant logic out of which true crime operates;[17] rather, it normalizes and even encourages female obsession with true crime.

This chapter takes a closer look at the intersection of true crime media and rape culture in the United States, drawing out its moral implications. To be clear, we are attending to media representations and public opinion not because they offer insight into how rape *should* be interpreted, but because they play an under-examined role in shaping how rape *is* interpreted. The research of criminologist Justin Pickett demonstrates that most members of the public are uninformed about criminal justice. Aggregate data (public opinion that is not segregated by demographic group) shows that the average American "thinks more than half of all [criminal] offenses are violent,"[18] and significantly overestimates their own risk of being a target of violent crime.[19] The primary influencer of public opinion (in the aggregate, to which policymakers pay the most attention) is the crime rate. That public opinion, in turn, shapes criminal justice policy by creating a "range of acceptable policies." According to Pickett, "the weight of the evidence also suggests that this relationship (public opinion around punitive policy and the crime rate) is mediated by changes in the number of news stories and the public's fear of crime."[20] In other words, mass media plays a major role in mediating public perception of crime, and subsequently, public policy.

Despite the fact that sexual violence is perceived as shameful and private, images of sexual violence "permeate almost every

---

[17] Ibid., 29.

[18] Justin T. Pickett, "Public Opinion and Criminal Justice Policy: Theory and Research," *Annual Review of Criminology* 2 (2019): 408.

[19] See Lincoln Quillian and Devah Pager, "Estimating Risk: Stereotype Amplification and the Perceived Risk of Criminal Victimization," *Social Psychology Quarterly* 73 (2010): 79–104.

[20] Pickett, "Public Opinion and Criminal Justice Policy," 416.

aspect of [Western] cultural life."[21] From the latest edition of *Runner's World* magazine to the Netflix series *13 Reasons Why*, representations of rape grace the pages of literary texts, magazines, music, talk shows, true crime documentaries, and major movies on a daily basis.[22] True crime media has capitalized on this phenomenon for the sake of entertainment.[23] This fascination within the context of true crime raises a number of serious moral questions: Why is watching violence against women so palatable? Why are people more curious about the lives of those who commit crimes than about their victims and survivors? What does our penchant for homicide cases reveal? Is sexual violence only relevant when the victims are dead? Is it only relevant when white women are assaulted? Why is there not the same curiosity and investment in telling the stories of the living, or in narrating survival and resistance to violence? The answers to these questions can give insight into how evil, hope, and moral agency are negotiated within public discourse.

DEFINING SEXUAL VIOLENCE

Survivors often give witness to a painful reality that their friends, family, and religious communities fail to recognize as sinful. Oftentimes, when survivors attempt to share what they have experienced, some of the most important people in their lives do not believe them. Many people struggle to see sexual

---

[21] Tanya Horeck, *Public Rape: Representing Violation in Fiction and Film* (New York: Taylor & Francis Group, 2003), 3.

[22] For example, see Christine Yo, "Women Deserve to Run without Fear," *Runner's World,* October 10, 2019; Larissa Brian, "After Steubenville: Incapacitated Bodies, Rape, and a Theory of Sexual Subjectivity beyond Consent," *Feminist Media Studies* 20, no. 2 (2020): 153–67.

[23] The voyeurism of raped unconscious women is hardly a new phenomenon. In the United States, it can be traced back to chattel slavery. See M. Shawn Copeland, *Knowing Christ Crucified: The Witness of African American Religious Experience* (Maryknoll, NY: Orbis Books, 2018), 96–101.

violence as a crime, much less as one worth punishing—according to RAINN (Rape, Abuse & Incest National Network), less than 3 percent of rapes committed and reported lead to a felony conviction.[24] And those are only the rapes that are reported; most are not (an estimated 70 percent).[25] As Lyndsie will discuss in greater detail in the following chapter, the reasons for not reporting are complex, and can range from fear to shame. Living in a climate that is hostile to survivors of rape does not help. Rape myths normalize a number of erroneous beliefs, including that rape is only committed by strangers; women who are assaulted were asking for it; when men become sexually aroused, they cannot control themselves; and it only counts as sexual assault if the woman is physically injured. As communication scholars Rosemary Pennington and Jessica Birthisel point out, these myths have been supported and reinforced by religious, legal, and social norms.[26] As ethicist Marvin Ellison explains, stigma "is often invoked around sex and sexuality such that a purity/pollution dichotomy differentiates those who are considered normal/good/clean from the spoiled/dangerous/and dirty."[27] This kind of sexual and spiritual hierarchy often appears in the form of commonsense knowledge, but is very rarely named explicitly. A classic example of this dichotomy is the idea that a young woman who has "lost" her virginity is "spoiled" or less pure. In the case of sexual violence and Christian tradition, such thinking can all too easily translate into religious justification for victim blaming.

---

[24] This statistic is an approximation that combines information from multiple federal government reports. RAINN, "The Criminal Justice System: Statistics," *Rape, Abuse & Incest National Network*, 2021, www.rainn.org.

[25] According to the National Crime Victimization Survey (NCVS), the percent of rape/sexual assault victimizations reported to police was 24.9 percent in 2018 and 33.9 percent in 2019. Rachel E. Morgan and Jennifer L. Truman, "Criminal Victimization, 2019," *Bureau of Justice Statistics* (September 2020).

[26] Pennington and Birthisel, "When New Media Make News," 2348.

[27] Marvin Ellison, *Making Love Just: Sexual Ethics for Perplexing Times* (Minneapolis: Fortress Press, 2012), 30–31.

Sexual violence refers to a broad spectrum of activities that may or may not be associated with criminality. The World Health Organization defines sexual violence as "any sexual act, attempt to obtain a sexual act, unwanted sexual comments or advances, or acts to traffic, or otherwise directed, against a person's sexuality using coercion, by any person regardless of their relationship to the victim, in any setting, including but not limited to home and work."[28] The *National Intimate Partner and Sexual Violence Survey* reports that about one in three women and nearly one in six men are affected by sexual violence.[29] Although it is difficult to acquire definitive statistics for sexual violence due to the lack of reporting, variations in definitions for sexual assault and rape, and different reporting requirements across jurisdictions, it remains a global issue that causes significant trauma.[30]

While sexual violence occurs among individuals, the root of the problem is social inequality and the ideologies of race, gender, class, and sexual supremacy that sustain it.[31] In heteropatriarchal cultures wherein masculinity is marked by aggression and femininity is marked by vulnerability, sexuality and violence can elide and normalize intimate partner violence. The notion that male conquest of women is expected, sexy, and desirable (without their consent) plays into ideation of sexual supremacy and hegemonic masculinity. This kind of socialization happens early in a person's life; violence is eroticized in iconic Disney movies geared toward children and in Hollywood feature films

---

[28] Etienne G. Krug, Linda L. Dahlberg, James A. Mercy, Anthony B. Zwi, and Rafael Lozano, eds., *World Report on Violence and Health* (Geneva: World Health Organization, 2002), 149.

[29] *National Intimate Partner and Sexual Violence Survey*, "Infographic on Intimate Partner Violence, Sexual Violence, and Stalking," Centers for Disease Control and Prevention, 2016.

[30] See the RAINN website to learn more about statistics related to reporting and convictions. The site also provides the laws for each state that address the differences in the legal definition of rape and the statute of limitations.

[31] Ellison, *Making Love Just*, 87.

for older audiences. Moreover, the normalization of heterosexual relationships can make it difficult for LGBTQ persons to identify and recognize intimate partner violence in various formulations. Survivors often fail to seek help because they minimize the impact of what has happened to them or the behaviors of the person who assaults them.[32] As communities, we turn a blind eye, not wanting to address or even acknowledge intimate violence, until it gets completely out of hand.[33] That is, too few people are willing to acknowledge the existence of intimate violence until bruises and broken bones appear.

STEUBENVILLE, OHIO, AND *ROLL RED ROLL*

A number of these issues come to the fore in the Netflix true crime documentary *Roll Red Roll*.[34] As the narrative is laid out in the film, on the night of August 11, 2012, students from Steubenville High School and surrounding schools attended numerous parties. Throughout the evening, students were posting to social media and texting each other. The next day a female, Jane Doe,[35] remembers little from the night and finds out through pictures and intimidating text messages that she has been sexually assaulted. There were numerous witnesses to the events that occurred that night, but no one stepped up to stop what was happening. Instead, the multiple football players assaulting Jane Doe took photos of her exposed body, posted videos expressing

---

[32] See Kathryn Holland and Lilia M. Cortina, "'It Happens to Girls All the Time': Examining Sexual Assault Survivors' Reasons for Not Using Campus Supports," *American Journal of Community Psychology* 59, no. 1 (2017): 50–64.

[33] Marie Fortune, *Sexual Violence: The Sin Revisited* (Cleveland: Pilgrim Press, 2005), 64.

[34] *Roll Red Roll,* directed by Nancy Schwartzman (Multitude Films, 2018), Netflix.

[35] The digital activist group Anonymous has used the name Jane Doe to refer to the survivor in this case. The film *Roll Red Roll* applies this term as well.

"she's dead," and tweeted, "The song of the night is 'Rape Me' by Nirvana." As the film explains, by August 14 Jane Doe was taken to the hospital and her parents shared the social media evidence with the police. Following the police investigation, Trent Mays and Ma'lik Richardson were accused and convicted of raping Jane Doe.

The film *Roll Red Roll* focuses on the aftermath of Jane Doe's sexual assault by multiple football players, taking on the issue of rape culture and how it divided the town. As recounted by the local DJ in the film:

> All I can tell you is this. It's a she/he said without a doubt. You know anybody can make an allegation. These girls, at these parties, sometimes maybe drink a little bit too much. Sometimes, they get a little promiscuous. . . . It's easier to tell your parents that you were raped, than, "Hey mom, dad, I got drunk and decided to let three guys have their way with me."

As illustrated in the quote above, Jane Doe is *held responsible for her own assault* (victim blaming) because she was "too promiscuous" and too drunk, but *consent was assumed when none was given*. The DJ calls her *credibility* into question by implying that Jane Doe would rather lie to her parents about being raped than tell them she had sex with multiple partners.[36] Finally, e*mpathy for the perpetrators* is evoked when the town is more concerned with the football players' careers than the survivor's well being.

This case foregrounds the complex relationship of true crime media and sexual violence. Initially, it was true crime blogger and former Steubenville resident Alexandria Goddard who brought

---

[36] For a discussion of the complexities of consent surrounding the Steubenville High School rape case, see Larissa Brian, "After Steubenville: Incapacitated Bodies, Rape, and a Theory of Sexual Subjectivity Beyond Consent," *Feminist Media Studies* 20, no. 2 (2020): 153–67.

the case to light and played a key role in recovering evidence. As reported in *Roll Red Roll*, Goddard pulled the roster of football players, went to their social media accounts, and captured a timeline of what happened that evening. Her blog caught the attention of the activist group Anonymous. Despite good intentions, all of this was done without the consent of the survivor.[37]

Jane Doe was commodified in the court proceedings and was rendered invisible in the media coverage surrounding her own case. While many stories featured quotes from the judge or social media, news reporting did not cover Jane Doe's own testimony. Headlines like "CNN Grieves That Guilty Verdict Ruined 'Promising' Lives of Steubenville Rapists," and "Steubenville Rape Case Splits Town between Big Red and Guy Fawkes,"[38] framed the situation as an example of tension between football culture and technological surveillance.[39] This is all too often the case in crime writing. In a great deal of true crime, the lives of survivors are unknown and unnarrated, appearing without context or concrete discussion of the sexual violence they endured. The survivors rarely get to speak for themselves; instead, they are on display, "postmortem and subject to spectorial dominance."[40] We do not hear their stories or learn about their futures. Instead, the audience is "invited to respond to a cast of predominantly white male characters based on their 'likeability (or lack thereof) . . . as cultural heroes or villains.'"[41] The plot revolves around "pragmatic and logistic circumstances of murder

[37] Pennington and Birthisel, "When New Media Makes News," 2441. Also see Erik Wemple, "CNN Is Getting Hammered for Steubenville Coverage," *Washington Post,* March 18, 2013.

[38] Big Red is the name of Steubenville High School's sports teams; Guy Fawkes was an infamous British conspirator.

[39] See Wemple, "CNN Is Getting Hammered for Stuebenville Coverage."

[40] Heather Nunn, "Silent Witness: Detection, Femininity, and the Postmortem Body," *Feminist Media Studies* 3, no. 2 (2003): 196–98. Also see Horeck, *Justice on Demand,* 132.

[41] Horeck, *Justice on Demand,* 161.

and on putting together the minute scraps of evidence that killers leave behind."[42] This approach reinforces a worldview in which violence is unpredictable, narrowly focused on the worst kinds of crimes, and in which the narrative is preoccupied with order, safety, and criminal justice.

There are many larger moral questions embedded in this case. Why is it so difficult to believe women in the first place? When is it okay for people outside the community to intervene, such as Goddard or the digital activist group Anonymous?[43] What happens to Jane Doe? How does she heal? What about Trent Mays and Ma'lik Richardson? What resources are they given for healthy reintegration and identity formation within the community? What about the families of everyone involved? While the film, in conjunction with the lesson plans it offers, does a fairly good job of focusing on masculinity, the number of people who *speak for and about* Jane Doe, without her consent, is deeply problematic.[44] *Roll Red Roll* replays Jane Doe's rape on-screen without posing any concrete solutions to rape culture. Moreover, no one in the film explicitly addresses what constitutes consent.[45] Similar questions can be asked of podcasts like MFM and *Serial*.[46] In MFM, Kilgariff and Hardstark use humor to contest rape culture (that is, the notion that good

---

[42] Jean Murley, *The Rise of True Crime: 20th Century Murder and Popular Culture* (Westport, CT: Praeger, 2008), 131–32.

[43] For more on this, see "Anonymous Comes to Town: The Hackers Who Took on High School Sexual Assault in Ohio," April 18, 2019, YouTube video.

[44] In the film, the producer indicates that Jane Doe's absence is to protect her identity.

[45] Horeck makes a similar claim in relationship to *Serial* Season 1. See Horeck, *Justice on Demand*, 137.

[46] *My Favorite Murder* has been critiqued in some media outlets; however, these observations rarely make it into mainstream media, and most critiques take place on social media platforms. To list just a few: Ashley Duchenmin, "White Women Need to Do Better: The Death of My Favorite Murder," *Bitch Media*, August 8, 2017; and DenHoed "The *My Favorite Murder* Problem."

girls don't have sex and don't take up space).[47] But while MFM does create space for expanding traditional gender boundaries and raises awareness of rape culture, media scholar Tanya Horeck questions its practical effect.[48] As she indicates, MFM centralizes white women's experiences of sexual violence. While violence against sex workers and LGBTQ persons do appear on episodes, they are far from being the norm. Shows like *Serial* regularly fail to contextualize crimes with the broader landscape of homicide statistics in the United States. They also omit important details, such as the fact that the victim's family did not consent to the podcast's production.[49] Finally, the true crime genre's emphasis on solving real crimes, while positioning viewers as amateur detectives, creates a dynamic where women's dead bodies become pawns in the contest for viewership and ratings.[50]

For survivors of sexual violence, retelling one's story can be empowering. Yet, few media producers have considered the potential retraumatizing impact of having one's story replayed over and over without one's consent. This is particularly the case when survivors do not have control over how or when their story is told.[51] Trauma-informed care involves empowering women and men who have experienced violence. Consent and agency are key aspects of the implementation of trauma-informed processes. Therefore, when true crime media producers fail to collaborate

---

[47] *My Favorite Murder with Karen Kilgariff and Georgia Hardstark,* "61—Live at the Neptune," podcast.

[48] Horeck, *Justice on Demand,* 131. See Horeck for a fuller analysis of MFM and *Serial* Season 1.

[49] Ibid., 137.

[50] Ibid., 132.

[51] D. Elliott et al., "Trauma-informed or Trauma-denied: Principles and Implementation of Trauma-informed Services for Women," *Journal of Community Psychology* 33 (2005): 461–77; Janice Carello and Lisa D. Butler, "Potentially Perilous Pedagogies: Teaching Trauma Is Not the Same as Trauma-informed Teaching," *Journal of Trauma and Dissociation* 15 (2014): 153–68.

with survivors or do not acknowledge or minimize the harm done to survivors, they do more harm than good.

THEODORE "TED" BUNDY

Theodore "Ted" Bundy is one of the most notorious serial killers. He is responsible for the murder of at least thirty females across numerous states, crimes he committed between 1974 and 1978. His victims were usually found strangled or with blunt-force head trauma. Bundy preyed on attractive young women, usually college aged, although some of his victims were significantly younger. He used various techniques to lure unsuspecting females to his vehicle, such as imitating a police officer or pretending to be injured and needing help. In January 1989 he was executed. By the time of his execution, he had become a household name, "synonymous with the term 'psychopath.'"[52]

In recent years there has been increased examination of Bundy, his crimes, and the women in his life. In 2019, Netflix portrayed his story in *Extremely Wicked, Shockingly Evil and Vile*, while in 2020 Amazon created an original docuseries, *Ted Bundy: Falling for a Killer*. There have also been numerous books, podcasts, and shows throughout the years that have told his story from various perspectives.[53] In each of them, Bundy is depicted

---

[52] Sarah Marshall, "The End of Evil," in *Unspeakable Acts: True Tales of Crime, Murder, Deceit, and Obsession*, ed. Sarah Weinman (New York: HarperCollins, 2020), 172.

[53] To date, he has been featured in over forty-five televised episodes, most of them posthumously, including *Ted Bundy: An American Monster* (2017); *Ted Bundy: The Devil in Disguise* (2017); *Murder Made Me Famous* (2015); *Ted Bundy: Serial Monster* (2018–2019); *Ted Bundy: Falling for a Killer* (2020); and *Conversations with a Killer: The Ted Bundy Tapes* (2019). He is also the subject of numerous books and a handful of feature-length films. Examples include Ann Rule, *The Stranger beside Me: The Shocking Inside Story of Serial Killer Ted Bundy* (New York: Norton, 1980); *The Stranger beside Me*, directed by Paul Shapiro (USA Cable Network, 2003); and *The Riverman*, directed by Bill Eagles (Koch Company: 2004), A & E network.

as an affable, handsome man, with a promising career in government and law ahead of him.[54] Many narratives feature interviews
with former friends and colleagues who attest on screen to his
upstanding character. As his longtime girlfriend Elizabeth (Liz)
Kendall reflected in her memoir, *The Phantom Prince: My Life
with Ted Bundy*, "By writing in the book that Ted was warm and
loving and lovable, I was avoiding facing the painful truth that I
knew only a small part of Ted."[55]

As time has passed, Bundy's mystique has only increased.
On screen, he is portrayed as a cunning criminal mastermind.
He outwits law enforcement and overpowers women through
brute force, and thus embodies a number of characteristics of
toxic masculinity. As Bundy describes himself in *Conversations
with a Killer*:

> A person of this type chooses his victims for a reason. His
> victims are young attractive women. Women are posses-
> sions. Beings which are subservient, more often than not,
> to males. Women are merchandise. From the pornographic,
> through *Playboy,* right on up to the evening news. So there
> is no denying the sexual component. However, sex has
> significance only in the context of a much broader scheme
> of things. That is possession, control, violence.[56]

At its root, toxic masculinity is about men feeling entitled to
exercise domination over people.

---

[54] *Conversations with a Killer: The Ted Bundy Tapes*, produced by Joe Berlinger
(RadicalMedia 2019), Netflix, S1:E1 "Handsome Devil," at 26:57.

[55] Elizabeth Kendall, *The Phantom Prince: My Life with Ted Bundy* (New York:
Abrams, 2020), 171. In early books about Ted Bundy, fake names such as Meg
Anders were used to protect Kendall's privacy. She originally shared her story
in 1981 using the pseudonym Elizabeth Kendall rather than her true name,
Elizabeth Kloepfer. In Rule's *The Stranger beside Me*, the name Meg Anders is
used for Bundy's girlfriend Elizabeth (Kloepfer) Kendall.

[56] *Ted Bundy Tapes*, S1:E2 "One of Us," at 1:22.

Moreover, stories portray Bundy as more charming and handsome than he really was, and in part this is why Zac Efron was selected to play him in the Netflix dramatization—after it was released, Netflix reportedly attempted to quash the rising tide of viewers proclaiming Ted Bundy "hot" online.[57] On TikTok and YouTube young white female users pretended to be getting ready for a date with Bundy, "only to lay on the floor and be dragged off screen as if they've been killed in the following frame."[58] Other posts show users dressing up as Bundy, on the hunt for his "victims." This is consistent with cultural responses at the time of his trial. Throughout his trials and even after he was sentenced to death, Bundy attracted women who supported him morally and financially.[59] Irrespective of intent, such responses serve to enliven victim-blaming culture by romanticizing violence against women and exploiting it to gain notoriety.[60]

Indeed, sparse attention has been given to Bundy's victims, survivors, and their families. Those who did survive often express feelings of shame and guilt. For years Liz Kendall remained quiet, initially regretting going to the police with her suspicions about Ted's involvement in local disappearances. In 2017, she became aware of an upcoming movie about Ted that was to be told from the girlfriend's perspective. She contacted the filmmakers and began collaborations with them; the film became *Extremely Wicked, Shockingly Evil and Vile,* starring Zac Efron. Kendall and her daughter, Molly, further felt it was important to update the book *The Phantom Prince* in order to tell the story in their own words. This also led them to participate

[57] Chloe Laws, "Can the Internet Please Stop Romanticizing Killers?" *Cosmopolitan*, February 4, 2019.

[58] Abby Lee Hood, "TikTok Has a Ted Bundy Problem," *MTV News*, August 13, 2019.

[59] David Schmid, *Natural Born Celebrities: Serial Killers in American Culture*, new ed. (Chicago: University of Chicago Press, 2005), 212.

[60] Ibid.

in the 2020 Amazon documentary series *Ted Bundy: Falling for a Killer.*[61]

In the docuseries *Conversations with a Killer: The Ted Bundy Tapes* (2019) and in the 2019 Netflix dramatization, the viewer is told comparatively little about the women Ted murdered.[62] In the *Ted Bundy Tapes,* we learn through voice-overs and news footage that Lynda Ann Healy, a college student at the University of Washington, disappeared in the middle of the night.[63] The viewer is shown newspaper clippings, bloody sheets, and pictures of her bones; this is interspersed with home videos from Ted's childhood. Similarly, *Extremely Wicked* narrates the crimes through voice-overs from news reports discussing the missing and murdered women, while the video displays Ted, Liz, and her daughter, Molly, having fun together, celebrating birthdays and riding bikes. The stark visual contrast places Ted Bundy at the optic center of the narrative and belittles the long-term impact of the trauma felt by the families, reducing the living memory of their loved ones to merely being one of Bundy's victims.

Extremely Wicked invites the audience to imagine Chi Omega sorority sister Lisa Levy in her final brutalized state through the retelling by the district attorney to the jury: "Lying face down in her blood. Her neck had been twisted at an inhuman angle. The jaw was broken. She was missing a nipple. Her body had bite marks on it. She'd been raped and strangled. Strangled with a pantyhose garrote, so tight that her neck was constricted to half its size." The inclusion of gruesome details like this are common

---

[61] See Kendall, *Phantom Prince*, ix.

[62] *Ted Bundy Tapes*, S1: E1.

[63] Police also made assumptions about the women he killed. When investigating the homicide of Lynda Healy, police assumed that her blood-soaked mattress and pillow were the result of a nosebleed or menstruation. They had ruled out "the possibility of foul play: 'Because they assumed Lynda Healy was possibly having her period at the time of her disappearance,' wrote Bob Keppel, the King County detective. . . . They assumed no kidnapper would want to have to sex with her.'" Marshall, "The End of Evil," 174–75.

within true crime narratives; their inclusion "reflects audience expectations and desires for murder to contain such elements as mystery, intrigue, profound aberrance, the discovery of hidden or 'secret' elements of a person's life, psychosexual drama, and the unvarnished portrayal of such human failings as greed, envy or lust. . . . The result is to make murder—which is often sordid and enacted for petty reasons . . . interesting in some way."[64] Such dramatizations and reenactments not only sanction voyeurism, but they also romanticize sexual violence and homicide. In the description of Lisa Levy, producers combine what happened to Levy and another woman, Margaret Bowman, into a single account.[65] The effect is one of accentuating the monstrosity of Bundy's crimes, further placing him outside the bounds of humanity (Levy was found raped, with her nipple bitten off; Bowman was found raped, strangled with pantyhose).

This is consistent with the representation of the figure of the psycho/sociopath in popular culture, in which the serial killer personifies "evil as hidden, persistent, [and] spectacularly gruesome."[66] Within this framework, sexual violence is depicted as the behavior only of dangerous psychopaths,[67] not "ordinary" people viewers might encounter in their lives or even have a relationship with. In both *Extremely Wicked* and *The Ted Bundy Tapes*, we see titillating evidence of the aftermath of Bundy's crimes through blood-stained sheets, skeletal remains, and body bags. Detectives, investigative reporters, and former legal counsel reflect upon their experiences with Ted and attest to his genius

---

[64] Murley, *True Crime*, 128.

[65] For more details, see Rule, *The Stranger beside Me*, 328–31.

[66] Murley, *True Crime*, 5.

[67] Megan McCabe, "Relationships instead of Hooking Up? Justice in Dating," in *Sex, Love, and Families: Catholic Perspectives*, ed. Jason King and Julie Hanlon Rubio (Minneapolis: Liturgical Press, 2019), 29. McCabe is citing Lynn M. Phillips's *Flirting with Danger: Young Women's Reflections on Sexuality and Domination* (New York: New York University Press, 2000).

in subverting the system. We hear from Ted's former friends and
family, who attest to his character, charm, and intelligence. Liz
Kendall, his ex-girlfriend, reflects upon the care he gave her
daughter, Molly. Yet, the viewer is never shown the impact of
these crimes on the families and communities of those victimized.[68] Nor are Bundy's homicides contextualized in light of
current statistics on American crime[69]; the focus remains solely
on Bundy and law enforcement. In this way, *Extremely Wicked* and
The Ted Bundy Tapes allow producers to "both sanitize murder and
have more control over the reality that they present."[70]

In *The Ted Bundy Tapes*, after sentencing Bundy to death for
"vile and heinous" crimes, Judge Edward Cowart says to him:
"You'd have made a good lawyer. I'd have loved to have you
practice in front of me. But you went the wrong way, partner."[71]
True crime viewers are often astonished when they see Bundy
escape from police custody twice due to lax supervision and
superior cunning. But the viewer does not see the excessive
privileged treatment he is given, as there is no side-by-side
comparison with treatment of the general prison population. For
instance, people held on charges of homicide are not allowed
unsupervised access to law libraries or unrestricted use of the

---

[68] However, the docuseries *Falling for a Killer* (2020) does interview the
friends and family members of those deceased. It also interviews survivor Carol
DaRonch. As Jennifer Baldwin explains in *Trauma-Sensitive Theology: Thinking
Theologically in the Era of Trauma* (Eugene, OR: Cascade, 2018), 33, secondary
trauma can reach the same symptomatic intensity as primary trauma.

[69] According to the most recent FBI statistics, violent crime (murder, rape,
robbery, and aggravated assault) account for 14 percent of total reported offenses
in 2018. The majority of offenses reported fell under the category of property
damage. And within the category of violent crime, murder makes up 1 percent
of all reported offenses. FBI Uniform Crime Reporting Statistics 2018.

[70] Murley, *True Crime*, 126.

[71] *Ted Bundy Tapes*, S1: E4, "Burn Bundy Burn." This also appears in the
obituary of Judge Coward printed in the national edition of the *New York Times*,
August 4, 1987, with the headline: "Edward D. Cowart, 62, Judge in Florida
Trial of Ted Bundy."

phone.[72] Producers deliberately eliminate this information so as to play off of American fears that "dangerous criminals [are] literally getting away with murder."[73] This is part of what makes the serial killer so scary in television shows. Such framing tactics also reinforce a racist heteropatriarchal worldview in which white women are at the epicenter of violent homicide and in need of dire protection because danger might be lurking around every corner. In so doing, such narratives reveal the depths of white allegiances to power through the racially informed cultural script of stranger danger.

The Bundy films play into a larger motif within the true crime genre that depicts violence, in general, and sexual assault in particular, as random, unpredictable, and gruesome. Stranger danger is a racialized script as it shapes the direction of emotional energy (care, compassion, anxiety) and praxis. At a young age, children learn which bodies it is okay to be near, which bodies are out of place.[74] Part of the cultural affective script for white women is learning to see ourselves as "endangered bodies," in need of protection from "*dark* shadowy" strangers. The cultural affective script of stranger informs moral and ethical decisions. Feminist philosopher Sara Ahmed explains:

> I remember a policeman coming to our classroom one time, to teach us all about what they called "stranger danger." The police, in evoking the stranger, also gave me a body in which to deposit my anxiety. If the stranger could be anyone, the stranger was someone I recognized; somebody I could I look out for. [75]

---

[72] In June 1977 he was allowed to appear in his own defense and granted access to the Pitkin County jailhouse law library. The next year he shimmied through a hole in a jail cell.

[73] Murley, *True Crime,* 47.

[74] Ibid.

[75] Sara Ahmed, *Living a Feminist Life* (Durham, NC: Duke University Press, 2017), 24.

In the United States, narratives of stranger danger within the context of sexual violence and criminal justice cannot be disentangled from anti-Blackness. After the Civil War, Southern states enacted a series of laws (called the Black Codes) intended to limit the freedom of African Americans, which were followed by Jim Crow laws.[76] For example, vagrancy laws made it a crime to be unemployed and resulted in substantial fines. Failure to pay these fines, resulted in imprisonment and forced labor on plantations.[77] White people justified these laws on the grounds that Black people were "mentally inferior and incompetent to order their own lives; thus, subjection to White superiority was necessary."[78] White people also believed the control of Black men was necessary to protect white women (*Stephen v. State*, 1852).[79] "Southern White males invoked a paternalistic concern for White female chastity; as such lynching the accused not only would punish the Black offenders for their crimes, but would also spare fragile White women from having to testify about their trauma in a public courtroom."[80] Here, patriarchy and anti-Blackness come together to form a socio-religious and cultural landscape where white feminine virtue is linked to the

---

[76] The first slave codes were enacted in 1712 by planters in colonial South Carolina. My discussion here is limited to those enacted postbellum. For more see John K. Cochran et al., "Rape, Race, and Capital Punishment: An Enduring Cultural Legacy of Lethal Vengeance?" *Race and Justice* 9, no. 4 (2019): 385. It is worth noting that while enslaved persons could not own property, make contracts, sue, or be sued, they could be held criminally responsible for their conduct. As Cochran et al. point out, in terms of legal status, this reflects a double standard for personhood. Enslaved persons were treated as property with respect to rights but held accountable as persons with respect to criminal acts.

[77] Carol Anderson, *White Rage: The Unspoken Truth of Our Racial Divide* (New York: Bloomsbury, 2017), 22; 44.

[78] Cochran, "Rape, Race, and Capital Punishment," 386.

[79] Ibid. Also see Peter W. Bardaglio, "Rape and the Law in the Old South: 'Calculated to Excite Indignation in Every Heart.'" *The Journal of Southern History* 60, no. 4 (1994): 749–72.

[80] Cochran, "Rape, Race, and Capital Punishment," 389.

criminalization of Black people. As we discuss in more detail in Chapter 4, white fears about Black criminality are alive and well today. They continue to inform currents in response to rape and sexual assault in our legal system today.[81] For example, juries are more likely to assign the death penalty in a homicide case that also includes a rape where the victim is white and the accused is Black.[82]

WHY "RESCUE THE KILLERS"?

Tanya Horeck suggests that one of the reasons people enjoy watching "long-form true crime shows" is related to "the activity of passing judgment on guilt and innocence, of distinguishing the 'good' guys from the 'bad' guys," and she notes that "there is a strong sense that watching (or listening to) and 'interpreting' these accused men and sharing our affective responses to them through networked digital media actually counts for something."[83] In other words, she suggests that there is an inherent pleasure that can be derived from passing judgment on these cases and then sharing our reactions online with our friends. More than this, the true crime serial leads people to believe they are participating in something bigger than themselves, such as building community, passing information along to the police, and becoming more educated about a broken system. Murderino culture, associated with the podcast *My Favorite Murder,* is a good example of this. Yet, all of this comes at a great cost to survivors, victims, persons who are incarcerated, and their families.

---

[81] Kimberlé Crenshaw, "Whose Story Is It, Anyway? Feminist and Antiracist Appropriation of Anita Hill," in *Race-ing Justice, En-gendering Power: Essays on Anita Hill, Clarence Thomas, and the Construction of Social Reality*, ed. Toni Morrison (New York: Pantheon Books, 1992), 412.

[82] Cochran, "Rape, Race, and Capital Punishment," 394,

[83] Horeck, *Justice on Demand,* 155.

Within the true crime serial, the lead character is law enforcement, and all others play a supporting role. Therefore, the more
violent the crime and the more dangerous the criminal, the more
heroic law enforcement appears to be.[84] The easiest trope upon
which to act this out is that of the white female victim and a
stranger rapist. In the backdrop are invisible characters, who are
never explicitly mentioned on screen: the image of the Black
male sexual predator. Producers are relying upon racialized narratives that link Black bestiality and white women's purity (innocence). These narratives go all the way back to chattel slavery.
The white female body is marked out as cherished property
(Kelly Brown Douglas's term) and juxtaposed with criminalized,
hypersexualized, dangerous Black bodies.[85] Whiteness renders
the rape of white women plausible and visible because of the
historical association of whiteness with chastity and purity. This
trope is sloppy and lazy character development that perpetuates
dangerous stereotypes and elides critical thinking about the complexities of sexual violence as it appears in real life. We live in a
country that does not believe that survivors deserve justice unless
they are innocent, or "rape-able." As Lyndsie discusses further in
the next chapter, the moral integrity of survivors is often called
into question based upon social circumstances, looks, racial/
ethnic identity, or previous sexual history. True crime producers
take shortcuts and avoid addressing the complexities of these
issues on screen by using, almost exclusively, white women. It
is not an accident or coincidence that most true crime features
the cases of brutal rapes and homicides of white women. In so
doing, no political or moral demands are made of the viewer and
solutions are simple. All one has to do is call the police. Yet, there

---

[84] Color of Change Hollywood, *Normalizing Injustice: The Dangerous Misrepresentations That Define Television's Scripted Crime Genre* (The USC Annenberg
Norman Lear Center, January 2020), 34.

[85] Kelly Brown Douglas, *Stand Your Ground: Black Bodies and the Justice of
God* (Maryknoll, NY: Orbis Books, 2015), 40–42.

is something profoundly wrong when "women are victims, never perpetrators, never citizens with a larger responsibility than calling the cops."[86] While the genre claims to be honest and truthful, and it does present some factual information from real cases, it also fictionalizes, exaggerates, and constructs truth. Many of its consumers never question what they see on the screen. True crime reveals the depth of white allegiances. Considering that everyone has a limited amount of time, energy, and resources, the question remains: Why do white people, and white Christians, invest so much effort in "rescuing the killers"—to use womanist ethicist Emilie Townes's phrase?[87] Why do white Christians invest in protecting our "image," in trying to appear antiracist?

The story of Alex, my student from the beginning of this chapter, did not have a happy ending. She left the university, and I never heard from her again. I think about her often, and I wonder how she is doing. I also wonder how her life might have been different if our society was one in which women were believed. To be clear, believing women is not just a matter of validating the story of a single woman in court. It is about creating cultures that facilitate telling. Many survivors, like Alex, hesitate to talk about their experience because they are afraid that they will not be believed. Western culture conveys this message in multiple ways, including erotizing violence in the media; failing to hold those who have violated women and men accountable; and minimizing and ignoring the problem. Ultimately, Alex did tell other people about her experience because she needed help—her immediate concerns revolved around housing, physical safety, and the ability to graduate. Believing survivors requires more than this; it is about making an investment in healing.

---

[86] P. E. Moskowitz, "True Crime Is Cathartic for Women. It's Also Cop Propaganda," *Mother Jones*, May/June, 2020.

[87] Emilie Townes, *Womanist Ethics and the Cultural Production of Evil* (New York: Palgrave, 2007), 151, 154–55.

3

A SCIENTIFIC
EXAMINATION OF
SEXUAL VIOLENCE

"I am evidence that there is more to that box, there
is a human being there. It is not just a kit. This is a
person."

—Ericka Murria, "About the Film,"
I Am Evidence

True crime media focuses on the more egregious acts of sexual violence and overlooks the everyday occurrences. While I
(Lyndsie) was in school completing my forensic science degree,
I was often asked if the work was just like what people see on
CSI and other television shows. At the time, I was aware of
many scientific inaccuracies, but I did not pay much attention
to the overall frame. For example, *Forensic Files* includes a fairly
accurate depiction of forensic tools like DNA analysis, but by
only presenting solved cases, viewers garner an unrealistic expectation regarding case outcomes. In this chapter, I uncover
the more complex reality by examining a range of sexual assault
cases, from those that are never reported to the ones that make

it to DNA testing. I begin with factors that affect a survivor's
decision to report, then describe the process that takes place if
a survivor does report the incident. I also examine how police
decisions influence investigations in relation to the rape kit
backlog, as well as what role forensic DNA can have in sexual
assault investigations.

REPORTING

After a sexual assault or other form of sexual violence incident
occurs, survivors face the difficult decision of whether or not to
report. Statistics on the Rape, Abuse & Incest National Network
(RAINN) website indicate that only 310 out of 1,000 sexual
assaults are reported.[1] There are many reasons why survivors do
not report in sexual assault cases; the decision-making process
for a survivor is complex and unique for each individual. Researchers have begun to examine and document the factors that
contribute to non-reporting, such as survivor fears, a culture
of victim blaming, failures in structural systems, and historical
victimization specifically of Black, Indigenous, and other people
of color (BIPOC) communities. The information and studies
presented in this chapter provide an overview of various factors
but are not a definitive list, nor do they encompass all of the
complexities associated with the decision-making process. Additionally, the research presented largely focuses on violence against
heterosexual women. This is not meant to diminish the realities

---

[1] Reporting statistics vary greatly based on the source. For the purposes of
this chapter, the RAINN website is used to exemplify the disparity between
reported and non-reported cases. The statistics reported by RAINN are based
on a variety of government and academic research studies. They are updated
annually and as more research is published. "The Criminal Justice System:
Statistics," RAINN, 2021.

of sexual violence against men or the LGBTQI community, but rather to allow a comparison between common media depictions and real-life situations.

Recall Alex's story from Chapter 2. As a survivor of intimate partner violence, she faced the difficult decision of whether or not to report what had happened to her. In order to report, she must first recognize the actions of her partner as sexual violence. As survivor Elise Roberts describes, it was difficult to identify what was happening as abuse. She states, "I was only 17. I just thought this is what relationships were. I didn't know any better. I knew that he was hurting me, but I didn't know how to talk about what was happening."[2] In the United States, CDC data indicates that over 40 percent of women experience some form of sexual violence during their lifetime, with over one in three women experiencing a form of intimate partner violence.[3] Statistics also indicate that sexual violence permeates all races and ethnicities[4]; however, women of color experience disproportionally higher rates of assault compared to non-Hispanic white

---

[2] "Elise's Story," RAINN, 2020.

[3] Sharon G. Smith, Xinjian Zhang, Kathleen C. Basile, Melissa T. Merrick, Jing Wang, Marcie-jo Kresnow, and Jieru Chen, "The National Intimate Partner and Sexual Violence Survey: 2015 Data Brief–Updated Release" (Atlanta: National Center for Injury Prevention and Control, Centers for Disease Control and Prevention, 2018). For global data refer to the World Health Organization, *Global and Regional Estimates of Violence against Women: Prevalence and Health Effects of Intimate Partner Violence and Non-partner Sexual Violence* (Geneva: World Health Organization, 2013).

[4] "In the United States, an estimated 32.3% of multiracial women, 27.5% of American Indian/Alaska Native women, 21.2% of non-Hispanic Black women, 20.5% of non-Hispanic white women, and 13.6% of Hispanic women were raped during their lifetimes." Matthew J. Breiding, "Prevalence and Characteristics of Sexual Violence, Stalking, and Intimate Partner Violence Victimization—National Intimate Partner and Sexual Violence Survey, United States, 2011," *Morbidity and Mortality Weekly Report. Surveillance Summaries* 63, no. 8 (September 5, 2014): 1.

women.[5] This is further compounded by long-held sexualization stereotypes of Black women that can affect whether or not survivors of color are taken seriously, resulting in non-reporting.[6]

Research indicates that the leading reasons for not reporting include assault by an intimate partner, a survivor's use of alcohol or drugs, and a lack of injuries. Survivors also cite fear of violence escalation, lack of evidence, and feelings of shame or guilt as factors that influenced their reporting decision.[7] Beyond these primary reasons for not reporting, cultural influences may also affect a survivor's decision to report. There exists an even lower disclosure rate among Latina survivors, given cultural norms that place family well being above personal well being, oppose the sharing of personal information with strangers, and adhere to traditional gender roles and marriage beliefs.[8] Immigration status can also impact whether a survivor seeks help following sexual assault.[9]

The reasons for not reporting are further complicated when the survivor experiences sexual abuse as a child. Gail Gardner,

---

[5] Michele Black, Kathleen Basile, Matthew Breiding, Sharon Smith, Mikel Walters, Melissa Merrick, Jieru Chen, and Mark Stevens, "National Intimate Partner and Sexual Violence Survey: 2010 Summary Report" (Atlanta: National Center for Injury Prevention and Control, Centers for Disease Control and Prevention, 2011).

[6] Joel R. Anderson, Elise Holland, Courtney Heldreth, and Scott P. Johnson, "Revisiting the Jezebel Stereotype: The Impact of Target Race on Sexual Objectification," *Psychology of Women Quarterly* 42, no. 4 (2018): 461–76.

[7] Manon Ceelen, Tina Dorn, Flora S. van Huis, and Udo J. L. Reijnders, "Characteristics and Post-decision Attitudes of Non-Reporting Sexual Violence Victims," *Journal of Interpersonal Violence* 34, no. 9 (2019): 1961–77.

[8] Courtney E. Ahrens, Laura Carolina Rios-Mandel, Libier Isas, and Maria del Carmen Lopez, "Talking About Interpersonal Violence: Cultural Influences on Latinas' Identification and Disclosure of Sexual Assault and Intimate Partner Violence," *Psychological Trauma: Theory, Research, Practice, and Policy* 2, no. 4 (2010): 284.

[9] Elizabeth Zadnik, Chiara Sabina, and Carlos A. Cuevas, "Violence against Latinas: The Effects of Undocumented Status on Rates of Victimization and Help-seeking," *Journal of Interpersonal Violence* 31, no. 6 (2016): 1141–53.

another survivor who shares her story on the RAINN website, explains that at five years old a family member began sexually abusing her. She also survived rape as an adult. For years, Gail never talked about the child abuse; then, after the adult incident, she reported to police and underwent a sexual assault forensic exam. She recalls:

> It was archaic. I was an African American woman who had been raped, which was not necessarily taken seriously at that time. I was taken to a bare hospital room that only had a tray of metal instruments in it. All of my clothes were taken away and I was only given a sheet to wear. It was freezing cold. They left me in there by myself for so long, just waiting. It was horrible. When the nurse finally came in, she started the exam without saying a word to me. The experience was awful—it was like being raped all over again.[10]

Gail's experience is an example of the potential secondary trauma or "second rape" survivors may face when seeking medical care.[11]

Often when a victim-survivor decides not to report, medical care is not sought either. Similar to high non-reporting rates, data indicates that the majority of survivors do not seek basic medical care.[12] Survivors may fear secondary victimization, victim blaming, and shame. Survivors who were threatened or harmed during a stranger rape were more likely to report the incident and seek medical care, while those who consumed

---

[10] "Gail's Story," RAINN, 2020.

[11] Rebecca Campbell, Sharon M. Wasco, Courtney E. Ahrens, Tracy Sefl, and Holly E. Barnes, "Preventing the 'Second Rape': Rape Survivors' Experiences with Community Service Providers," *Journal of Interpersonal Violence* 16, no. 12 (2001): 1239–59.

[12] Black et al., "National Intimate Partner and Sexual Violence Survey: 2010 Summary Report."

drugs and/or alcohol were less likely to seek care.[13] The fears and barriers related to seeking medical services are compounded for minority, impoverished, socially isolated, and undocumented women.[14] Prior to 2005, it was common for medical facilities to require reporting to police prior to a medical exam, but with the reauthorization of the Violence Against Women Act (VAWA), this funding could no longer require police reporting in order to cover the expenses of the forensic medical examination.[15] Studies have reported that survivors' concerns related to the legal process have deterred them from seeking medical treatment and indicate that outreach education efforts to promote post-assault healthcare can benefit survivors.[16] While this chapter focuses on the forensic implications of collecting sexual assault evidence, it is also important to recognize the long-term physical and emotional health-related effects suffered by survivors.[17]

THE PROCESS

In order to demystify the process of a sexual assault investigation, I will walk through the process while highlighting various

---

[13] Heidi S. Resnick, Melisa M. Holmes, Dean G. Kilpatrick, Gretchen Clum, Ron Acierno, Connie L. Best, and Benjamin E. Saunders, "Predictors of Post-Rape Medical Care in a National Sample of Women," *American Journal of Preventive Medicine* 19, no. 4 (2000): 214–19.

[14] Lauren Anne Acosta, "Exploring Cultural and Socio-Political Influences on the Post-Rape Decisions and Behaviors of Undocumented Immigrant Women of Mexican-Origin," PhD dissertation, University of Arizona, 2019.

[15] Violence Against Women and Department of Justice Reauthorization Act of 2005, H.R. 3402, 109th Cong. (2005–2006).

[16] Heidi S. Resnick et al., "Predictors of Post-Rape Medical Care in a National Sample of Women," 214–19; J. M. Zweig, L. Newmark, D. Raja, and M. Denver, *Sexual Assault Medical Forensic Exams and VAWA 2005* (Washington, DC: US Department of Justice, 2014).

[17] Black et al., "National Intimate Partner and Sexual Violence Survey: 2010 Summary Report." Data indicates a higher prevalence of adverse mental and physical health outcomes for individuals who have experienced sexual violence.

complications that may be encountered by survivors. If a survivor decides to report, they initiate an investigation by police. Alternatively, the survivor can decide to seek medical care without reporting the assault to the police. Medical care includes treatment of injuries and an evaluation of pregnancy and sexually transmitted infection (STI) risk, as well as access to counseling and mental health services.[18] In addition to receiving medical treatment and support services, the individual may choose to undergo an examination focused on evidence collection (using a sexual assault evidence kit). This medical forensic examination is used to collect and preserve evidence that may eventually be used as part of a criminal investigation. Typically, evidence collection occurs up to five days post assault, but as scientific technology continues to advance, research indicates the possibility of recovering DNA evidence beyond five days.[19]

Preferably, a trained professional such as a sexual assault nurse examiner or sexual assault forensic examiner performs the exam, which includes the documentation and collection of both biological and physical evidence. The importance of having trained personnel conducting the examination is twofold: (1) to ensure the exam is performed in a patient-centered, trauma-informed manner, which is best for the survivor; and (2) to ensure that proper evidence collection techniques are followed so as to maintain the integrity of evidence for future processing. The examination is an extremely invasive process that involves the collection of bodily fluids and other samples in order to gather evidence of the assault and to attempt to identify the person

---

[18] US Dept of Justice, Office on Violence Against Women, and United States of America, "National Protocol for Sexual Assault Medical Forensic Examinations: Adults/Adolescents" (2013); D. Di Nitto, P. Y. Martin, D. B. Norton, and M. S. Maxwell, "After Sexual Assault: Who Should Examine Sexual Assault Survivors?" *The American Journal of Nursing* 86, no. 5 (May 1986): 538–40.

[19] National Institute of Justice (NIJ), "National Best Practices for Sexual Assault Kits: A Multidisciplinary Approach" (2017).

who committed it. The survivor has complete autonomy to give or withhold consent to this process and may refuse or stop the examination at any time. The evidence collected is contained in the aforementioned sexual assault evidence kit (SAEK).[20] As described in Gail's story above, the sexual assault examination is a very invasive process that risks further traumatization. Updated protocols and guidance thus emphasize the need for trauma-informed care in order to limit potential re-traumatization.

In ideal circumstances, following collection, the kit is given to police and is then transferred to a forensic science laboratory for DNA testing, all the while maintaining the proper chain of custody. The goal of DNA testing is to identify the person who committed the crime. For example, finding the person of interest's DNA profile on the vaginal swab indicates contact between the two individuals. While DNA testing cannot prove or disprove consent, it can provide a tangible, indisputable link between the people involved. If there is a person of interest in the case, the DNA profile from that individual can be compared to the DNA profile developed from the evidence. If there is not a person of interest, the recovered evidence profile can be searched in a DNA database to find a potential match.[21] An example is the case of Ralph Skundrich, who in 2014 was sentenced to 75 to 150 years for rape after being identified in 2010 using the national DNA database. This conviction came twelve years after the incident, in which he broke into a Pittsburgh apartment and assaulted the survivor, who was eighteen at the time.[22] Another

---

[20] Ibid.

[21] NIJ, US Department of Justice, Office of Justice Programs, and United States of America, "Sexual Assault Kits: Using Science to Find Solutions" (2015).

[22] Ralph Skundrich was also connected to and convicted of a rape in Butler County, Pennsylvania, which occurred weeks before the Pittsburgh attack. Paula Reed Ward, "Man Sentenced to 75–150 Years for Rape," *Pittsburgh Post-Gazette*, April 18, 2014; "Judge to Man Sentenced in '02 Rape of Pittsburgh College Student: 'Your Days of Torturing Women Are Over,'" WTAE Pittsburgh, April 18, 2014.

example involves Debbie Smith, who was taken from her house and raped in her backyard on March 3, 1989. The individual who assaulted her was finally identified in 1995 through the national DNA database.[23] Her story led to legislation that aids in the processing of sexual assault kits. The Debbie Smith Act—originally passed in 2004 and most recently reauthorized in 2019—provides funding for DNA testing of sexual assault evidence kits.[24]

THE BACKLOG

The above examples demonstrate how reporting, investigating, and testing can result in a conviction, bringing some level of closure for the survivor. But even when survivors make the brave decision to report and undergo the sexual assault examination, hurdles remain, as exemplified by the nationwide rape kit backlog. In the late 1990s and early 2000s, the media brought widespread attention to the issue of untested sexual assault evidence kits in New York City, Los Angeles, and Detroit.[25] More recently, the 2017 HBO documentary *I Am Evidence* highlighted the issue of untested rape kits, primarily from the perspective of four survivors who shared their negative experiences with the investigation process.[26]

---

[23] "Debbie Smith Act," Hope Exists after Rape Trauma (H-E-A-R-T); and "Debbie Smith Act," RAINN, 2020.

[24] Debbie Smith Reauthorization Act of 2019, H.R. 777, 116th Congress (2019). DNA testing for one SAEK costs approximately $1,000–$2,000, but costs can vary greatly based on the jurisdiction and factors such as laboratory size, caseload, and resources. Paul J. Speaker, "The Jurisdictional Return on Investment from Processing the Backlog of Untested Sexual Assault Kits," *Forensic Science International: Synergy* 1 (2019): 18–23.

[25] Rebecca Campbell, Giannina Fehler-Cabral, Steven J. Pierce, Dhruv B. Sharma, Deborah Bybee, Jessica Shaw, and B. A. Feeney, "The Detroit Sexual Assault Kit (SAK) Action Research Project (ARP), Executive Summary" (Washington, DC: US Department of Justice, 2015).

[26] *I Am Evidence*, directed by Trish Adlesic and Geeta Gandbhir (HBO Documentary Films, 2017). See also https://www.iamevidencethemovie.com/.

The testing backlog serves as a tangible example of the lack of due recognition placed on sexual assault investigations. Media outlets use the term *backlog* to refer to sexual assault evidence kits that are unsubmitted and stored in police facilities or awaiting testing at the laboratory.[27] While in technical terms there is a formal difference between unsubmitted and backlogged kits, for the purposes of this book, we also use the term *backlog* to represent any kit that has not been tested. The issue of unsubmitted and backlogged kits is a national problem caused by numerous factors. For example, police may doubt the evidentiary value of the kit, the credibility of the survivor, and/or the seriousness of the assault, resulting in the kit never being submitted to the laboratory.[28] The backlog is a twofold issue: either kits were never submitted to forensic laboratories based on police decisions, or kits were submitted but not tested by the laboratories. If the survivor decides not to file a police report, the kit will likely sit in storage, never to be tested.

Numerous jurisdictions identify victim blaming by law enforcement as a leading factor contributing to the test kit backlogs. One report detailing the examination of SAEKs in Detroit includes negative law enforcement sentiments documented in police reports and expressed during interviews between researchers and police such as "got what they got," "a deal gone bad," and "not really a rape."[29] Importantly, the negative sentiments police felt toward survivors often influenced their decision whether or not to submit kits for forensic analysis.[30] Rape myths specific to

---

[27] NIJ, "Sexual Assault Kits."

[28] Reasons to doubt the evidentiary value include the following: the person who committed the assault was known; the case was dismissed; testing was not requested by the prosecutor; or the survivor bathed prior to collection.

[29] R. Campbell, G. Fehler-Cabral, S. J. Pierce, D. Sharma, D. Bybee, J. Shaw, and H. Feeney, "The Detroit Sexual Assault Kit (SAK) Action Research Project (ARP)" (NIJ 2011–DN-BX-0001; NCJRS Document No. 248680) (Washington, DC: NIJ, 2015): 135–37.

[30] Ibid., 135–36, 295.

the survivor in a case show up in police reports, including language such as "victim didn't fight back; victim is lying; victim consented; victim is not injured; victim is not upset; victim is a sex worker; victim is a regular drug user."[31] Although there are numerous stereotypes and beliefs surrounding the characteristics of a "real rape," research shows the beliefs do not align with the majority of actual cases.[32] An example of a stereotypical "real rape" is one that occurs between strangers and involves the use of weapons or physical force.[33] This contrasts with data indicating that the majority of assaults involve an intimate partner, family member, friend, or acquaintance and do not involve a weapon.[34]

Submission of SAEKs varies drastically by police jurisdiction. One research study indicates a submission rate of only 19.2 percent for Illinois SAEKs collected from 1995 to 2010.[35] The location of the assault was also a leading factor in whether or not a kit was submitted; for example, in a Western state, between two neighboring counties, one county was 10 times more likely than the other to submit evidence within a year of the

---

[31] Jessica Shaw, Rebecca Campbell, Debi Cain, and Hannah Feeney, "Beyond Surveys and Scales: How Rape Myths Manifest in Sexual Assault Police Records," *Psychology of Violence* 7, no. 4 (2017): 605.

[32] Kimberly A. Lonsway, Joanne Archambault, and David Lisak, "False Reports: Moving beyond the Issue to Successfully Investigate and Prosecute Non-Stranger Sexual Assault," *The Voice* 3, no. 1 (2009): 1–11.

[33] Janice DuMont, Karen-Lee Miller, and Terri L. Myhr, "The Role of 'Real Rape' and 'Real Victim' Stereotypes in the Police Reporting Practices of Sexually Assaulted Women," *Violence Against Women* 9, no. 4 (April 2003): 466–86.

[34] Data from 2005 to 2010 indicate that in 78 percent of cases the individual who committed the assault is known to the survivor, and that a weapon was used in only 11 percent of sexual assaults. Marcus Berzofsky, Christopher Krebs, Lynn Langton, Michael Planty, and Hope Smiley-McDonald, "Female Victims of Sexual Violence, 1994–2010," *Bureau of Justice Statistics* (2013).

[35] Sarah Tofte, *I Used to Think the Law Would Protect Me: Illinois's Failure to Test Rape Kits* (New York: Human Rights Watch, 2010).

assault.[36] The different submission rates based on location of the assault reflect the highly subjective nature of law enforcement submission decisions.

Additional variables were found to statistically predict SAEK submission by police. For example, kits were less likely to be submitted if the survivor disclosed drug use prior to the assault, had bathed or showered, or suffered from a physical or mental impairment. Alternatively, kit submission was more likely if the incident was a potential drug-facilitated assault, if the person of interest was a stranger, or if the survivor was a male.[37] The Netflix miniseries *Unbelievable*, based on the real-life story of Marie Adler, highlights what can happen when police fail to believe survivors. Had a proper investigation followed Marie's assault, along with testing of the rape kit, future assaults by Marc O'Leary may have been prevented.[38]

In Marie's case, police believed she had falsely reported. It is impossible to assess accurately the true number of false reports that occur, and estimates are often inflated by relying only on detective narratives that determine the veracity of a report.[39] By examining methodological research studies, the estimates of false reports narrow to 2–10 percent.[40] But since false reporting is a

---

[36] Julie L. Valentine, L. Kathleen Sekula, Lawrence J. Cook, Rebecca Campbell, Alison Colbert, and Victor W. Weedn, "Justice Denied: Low Submission Rates of Sexual Assault Kits and the Predicting Variables," *Journal of Interpersonal Violence* 34, no. 17 (2019): 3547–73.

[37] Ibid.

[38] T. Christian Miller and Ken Armstrong, "An Unbelievable Story of Rape," *ProPublica* and *The Marshall Project* (December 16, 2015); T. Christian Miller and Ken Armstrong, *A False Report: A True Story of Rape in America* (New York: Crown Publishing Group, 2018); Ira Glass, host, "Anatomy of Doubt," podcast audio, *This American Life,* February 26, 2016.

[39] Eugene J. Kanin, "False Rape Allegations," *Archives of Sexual Behavior* 23 (1994): 81–91.

[40] Kimberly A. Lonsway et al., "False Reports: Moving beyond the Issue to Successfully Investigate and Prosecute Non-Stranger Sexual Assault," *Prosecutor, Journal of the National District Attorneys Association* 43, no. 1 (2009): 10–22;

sad reality—though not as pervasive as society and investigators might think—law enforcement must establish training and protocols that correctly investigate every case so that investigators do not misclassify a report.

Alternatively, even if police believe a crime occurred, they may not send the kit to the laboratory if the identity of the person who committed the assault is already known. While the identity may be known in one case, it may be unknown in others. For example, the Los Angeles Police Department (LAPD) and Los Angeles Sheriff's Department (LASD) received grant funding to examine the role of DNA testing on previously unsubmitted sexual assault kits. After DNA testing by the laboratory, some of the cases were eligible to be submitted to the DNA database CODIS (Combined DNA Index System). Database searching and case-to-case hits found that some cases involving a stranger could be linked to a case where the identity of the individual's DNA was known.[41] A hit indicates a potential DNA match between cases that is further confirmed through additional DNA testing.

Another example, in Cuyahoga County, Ohio, also shows that it's possible to connect known and unknown sexual assault cases. After testing nearly five thousand backlogged cases, some results indicated that the same individual committed intimate partner sexual assault as well as acquaintance and stranger assaults.[42] As we discussed earlier, intimate partner violence cases are rarely reported, and if they are, the individuals are known, which could influence the investigator's decision to submit forensic evidence

---

David Lisak et al., "False Allegations of Sexual Assault: An Analysis of Ten Years of Reported Cases," *Violence Against Women* 16, no. 12 (2010): 1318–34.

[41] Nancy Ritter, "Solving Sexual Assault: Finding Answers through Research," *NIJ Journal* 270 (June 2012): 4–17.

[42] Rachel E. Lovell, Cyleste C. Collins, Margaret J. McGuire, Laura T. Overman, Misty N. Luminais, and Daniel J. Flannery, "Understanding Intimate Partner Sexual Assaults: Findings from Sexual Assault Kits," *Journal of Aggression, Maltreatment and Trauma* 28, no. 1 (2019): 8–24.

for analysis. The case of Amberley, one of the stories featured in the *I Am Evidence* documentary, could possibly have been prevented had a sexual assault kit been processed two years earlier, when the same person attacked another teenager. If the kit from the earlier assault had been processed and led to an identification, Amberley's assault may not have happened.[43]

TESTING

As noted above, the sexual assault evidence kit can undergo forensic DNA testing in order to determine the identities of the individuals involved in the incident.[44] As an investigative tool, DNA evidence can connect individuals to a crime or exclude them from it. It can also assist prosecutors by increasing survivor credibility and corroborating a survivor's story; meeting the jurors' evidence expectations; countering defense arguments related to no-contact between the individuals; and securing plea agreements.[45] DNA testing of all kits can also identify individuals who have committed multiple assaults, as discussed earlier. Testing of SAEKs in Detroit showed increased database hits, thus connecting serial crimes.[46] The Detroit study, along with reports of backlog processing results in Los Angeles and Ohio, clearly indicate the importance of testing stranger-attacker and known-attacker kits.

---

[43] Amanda Holpuch, "I Am Evidence: The Shocking Film on the Truth about Untested Rape Kits," *The Guardian*, April 13, 2018.

[44] For a detailed explanation of the DNA analysis process, see NIJ, "DNA Evidence: Basics of Analyzing" (2012).

[45] Tri Keah S. Henry and Alicia L. Jurek, "Identification, Corroboration, and Charging: Examining the Use of DNA Evidence by Prosecutors in Sexual Assault Cases," *Feminist Criminology* 15, no. 5 (2020): 634–58.

[46] Forty-nine percent of kits tested resulted in a DNA profile that was eligible for upload to the national DNA database, CODIS. The 785 CODIS-eligible profiles resulted in 455 CODIS hits and evidence of 127 serial sexual assaults. Campbell et al., "The Detroit Sexual Assault Kit (SAK) Action Research Project (ARP)," vi.

Forensic DNA analysis can provide answers and closure, but it is impossible to test material that was never submitted.

The successful arrival of kits at forensic laboratories for testing still leaves multiple barriers. As described earlier, after the survivor formally files a report with law enforcement, the kit is transferred from the hospital to police custody. The police then decide whether to send the kit to the forensic laboratory. If they do send it, the laboratory then makes a testing decision based on resources and on whether there is a sufficient amount of DNA available for testing.

To recap: At this point, a survivor has endured the traumatic experience of sexual assault, undergone an invasive kit collection process, provided consent to have the kit sent forward for testing (which may require additional reporting to law enforcement), and now awaits further investigative updates from law enforcement, including the scientific results from forensic analysis of the kit. Again, this pathway illustrates the complex chain of events that can be set in motion for a survivor who chooses to report, have a kit collected, and agrees to testing.

Survivors who want their kits tested deserve to have them tested. The DNA technology exists to perform the testing, and while testing the kit does not guarantee a specific outcome in the criminal justice system, it can support the survivor and the community in seeking accountability. Advocates for improving accountability for sexual assault survivors propose a test-all approach for reported cases. In this scenario, all kits collected would be sent to the forensic laboratory for testing as long as the survivor provided consent for testing.[47] Although DNA results may be inconclusive following testing, mandatory testing renders moot any arguments law enforcement could make against submitting the test kits. Additionally, advocates argue that cases

---

[47] The Joyful Heart Foundation's End the Backlog Initiative, www.endthebacklog.org.

lacking current consent for testing should be maintained by law enforcement in order to uphold the survivors' right to have their kits tested in the future if they so choose.

The issue of survivor consent in testing and reporting plays an important role in test-all recommendations. Some jurisdictions specifically mandate that consent from the survivor is needed for the kit to proceed to the laboratory. Pennsylvania law outlines that within fifteen days of receiving written consent for testing, the evidence must be sent to the laboratory. The laboratory then has six months to complete analysis.[48] Any kit awaiting testing for twelve months or longer is reported as backlogged sexual assault evidence. The numbers of kits in the backlog represent kits that have consent for testing but have not undergone forensic testing.[49] At the end of 2020, Pennsylvania reported ninety-four kits in the backlog, a significant decrease from the three thousand backlogged kits in 2016.[50] At the federal level, in accordance with recommendations from the "National Best Practices for Sexual Assault Kits" report and the position of the national Office on Violence against Women, all kits with survivor consent to submission and reporting to law enforcement should proceed to forensic testing.[51] These recommendations further explore the ability of survivors to report anonymously, thereby facilitating consent to the process and allowing the kit to move forward for testing. Numerous alternative reporting options are being explored nationwide. One mechanism utilizes anonymous

---

[48] Commonwealth of Pennsylvania. Act of Jul. 10, 2015, P.L. 142, No. 27 Cl. 18—Sexual Assault Testing and Evidence Collection Act.

[49] Pennsylvania Department of Health, *Untested Sexual Assault Kits and Backlogged Evidence*, May 2020.

[50] Auditor General Eugene DePasquale, "Auditor General DePasquale: New State Data Show 97 percent Drop in Backlogged Rape Kits; Lowest Total in At Least Four Years," Pennsylvania Department of the Auditor General, May 5, 2020.

[51] NIJ, "National Best Practices; United States Department of Justice Office on Violence Against Women, "Sexual Assault Kit Testing Initiatives and Non-investigative Kits," White Paper, January 2017.

reporting where the survivor consents to kit collection, participation with investigators and other members of the criminal justice system, and kit testing, but remains anonymous throughout the entire process.[52] Multiple jurisdictions have enacted legislation requiring the testing of all reported SAEKs with testing consent in the hope of bringing accountability to survivors.[53]

Some jurisdictions and forensic laboratories struggle to meet testing demands due to limited resources; as a result, many laboratories must make difficult decisions when deciding which cases to test. The 2017 "National Best Practices for Sexual Assault Kits" report provides recommendations for direct-to-DNA analysis techniques that can conserve labor-intensive resources,[54] and there is some funding available, such as that provided by the Debbie Smith Act, that can provide resources for forensic crime laboratories to increase their DNA-processing capacity.[55] But forensic laboratories must continue to seek an ethical balance that fairly distributes resources in order to more widely promote justice, and the scientific community should also strive to improve testing methods and availability in order to ensure that all reported sexual assault kits undergo proper testing.

MOVING FORWARD

In this chapter, I have outlined the sexual assault investigation process with a specific focus on the SAEK backlog and the role of forensic DNA analysis. As a scientist, I focus on the available data, which clearly show a lack of reporting, testing, and convictions related to sexual assault cases. The reasons for this are complex

---

[52] NIJ, "National Best Practices."

[53] The Joyful Heart Foundation's End the Backlog Initiative. See, for example, CO Rev. Stat. § 24–33.5–113(4).

[54] NIJ, "National Best Practices."

[55] Debbie Smith Reauthorization Act of 2019, H.R. 777, 116th Congress (2019).

and multifaceted, but I believe there needs to be a broader shift in public perception related to sexual assault—our culture needs to eliminate victim blaming and work to help survivors heal while preventing future violence. In part, this could take the form of concentrated efforts by multidisciplinary teams to improve sexual assault investigations and prosecutions, but there are broader issues beyond the realm of investigators, scientists, and prosecutors. As discussed at the beginning of the chapter, the majority of survivors do not report, so the criminal justice system never becomes involved in the case at all—this means that there's no evidence collected, nothing to be forensically tested, and often no conclusion.

News headlines rush to condemn the rape kit backlog, but this is only part of the problem. I agree that the lack of testing of sexual assault evidence kits is a serious failure of the criminal justice system to provide closure for survivors; this failure is being addressed by the forensic science community and related criminal justice entities. Perhaps the larger issue, however, is that the number of kits is relatively small in comparison to the true number of assaults. Psychologist and researcher David Lisak laments that although sexual violence is regarded as a serious violent crime, second only to homicide, the number of cases actually reported and prosecuted are only a fraction of the actual number of sexual assaults that are committed.[56]

As discussed earlier, public and law enforcement views related to sexual assault cases largely consist of negative stereotypes and victim blaming. This by no means diminishes the fact that a problem does exist in relation to rape kit backlogs, but it is important to understand the broader picture. While DNA analysis can have an important impact on these cases, this still accounts for only a fraction of true assaults. Therefore, solutions to the larger systemic issues related to sexual assault cases must go beyond the work done in the laboratory.

[56] David Lisak, "Understanding the Predatory Nature of Sexual Violence," *Sexual Assault Report* 14, no. 4 (2008): 49–64.

The stereotypes about survivors of sexual assault are often related to implicit biases regarding the survivor's behavior and its consequences. For example, if a survivor was drinking alcohol, society may view the individual as responsible for the sexual assault. This behavior of victim blaming is harmful and problematic because it places survivors at fault for the sexual assault based on a choice they made or actions they took. This belief is incorrect. There is no specific choice or behavior that results in sexual activity; rather, the commonality in sexual assaults revolves around the decision of the individual to sexually assault another individual.[57] I'll explore the concept of bias further in Chapter 6.

As a former DNA analyst, I was trained to analyze evidence, such as the material included in sexual assault evidence kits, and to report the presence or absence of DNA. If DNA was present, the next step was to determine if that genetic material matched a person of interest. While the testing would allow me to determine the identity of the person whose DNA was present, the scientific analysis cannot indicate if an encounter was consensual or not. Even with this limitation, however, I believe it is necessary to process the evidence, regardless of the outcome, in order to uphold survivors' rights who have consented to the testing process and to validate the importance of the investigation and the seriousness of sexual assault crimes.

Finally, it is important to remember that every case of sexual violence, reported or not, has a human element. Although as a scientist I was trained to remain unbiased, the testing being performed has no meaning without the human connection. The swabs and other items collected in the sexual assault evidence kit represent the survivors. Human lives are drastically impacted by the work performed by myself and other forensic scientists. In forensic science we are tasked with contributing to the justice

---

[57] Heather Huhtanen, Kimberly A. Lonsway, and Joanne Archambault, "Training Bulletin Series Part 2: Gender Bias in Victim Blaming and Selection," End Violence Against Women International (November 2017), 11.

process by aiding investigations through evidence analysis and testifying about the results in court. But most sexual violence cases never make it to the criminal justice system, and even if they do there can be drastic differences between case outcomes. As indicated by low reporting, the vast majority of survivors live in silence and may struggle with lifelong physical and psychological effects from the assault. Cases of sexual violence are not anomalies, and all too often it is the depictions that do not appear in true crime media that are the most pervasive in our culture.[58]

---

[58] For one such example, the high rate of intimate partner violence, see Smith et al., "The National Intimate Partner and Sexual Violence Survey" (2018). Another example is the fact that Indigenous populations are most at risk of sexual violence, and that such cases are further complicated because 80 percent of the individuals who commit the assault are non-Indigenous and therefore immune from tribal court prosecution. See Louise Erdrich, "Rape on the Reservation," *ProQuest Historical Newspapers: New York Times*, February 27, 2013, A25.

4

SEXUAL HARASSMENT AND THE THEOLOGICAL ROOTS OF (DIS)BELIEF

In May 2019, thousands of McDonald's workers went on strike just days after the Fight For $15, American Civil Liberties Union, and TIME'S UP Legal Defense Fund announced they were bringing twenty-five sexual harassment charges and lawsuits against the company on behalf of workers nationwide. Like many large companies, McDonald's has a zero-tolerance policy for sexual harassment in the workplace.[1] The purpose of a zero-tolerance policy for workplace discrimination is to demonstrate that a company takes violence seriously. Yet, when it comes to policy and praxis, the issue is much more complex. Most workplace sexual harassment policies are designed to protect the employer (from liability) rather than the employee. Moreover, zero-tolerance policies often fail because they do

---

[1] National Women's Law Center (NWLC), "TIME'S UP Legal Defense Fund™ . . . Supports New Sexual Harassment Charges against McDonald's by Workers across the Country," press release, May 21, 2019.

not address root issues, such as toxic masculinity and white entitlement cultures.[2]

To illustrate the depths of the problem and common dynamics within workplace sexual harassment, let's turn to the story of nineteen-year-old Brittany Hoyos. As she narrates in *The Guardian*:

> I quickly learned how to deal with rude customers or keep the drive-thru moving. But I didn't know how to deal with the unwanted and uncomfortable attention from my older shift manager. He took opportunities to unnecessarily touch me or brush up against me. He would often text me inappropriate messages like how I looked good in my jeans. I tried to convince myself that this was just how things worked in the fast-food industry and that I needed to stay quiet if I wanted to keep my job.[3]

When the Hoyos family car was repossessed and her manager offered her rides home, Brittany accepted. One evening on the way home, her manager tried to kiss her. After Brittany rejected her manager's sexual advances, she was called names by him and by other coworkers. Ashamed, embarrassed, and unsure of what to do, Brittany kept quiet. When her family finally reported the incident, Brittany was "forced into a meeting with several managers, with her harasser present, where she was told to 'stop bringing up the past,' and to 'let it go.'"[4] After speaking out, Brittany and her mother, who was also an employee at the store, had their hours cut and were disciplined for minor infractions. Brittany was fired, and her mother resigned.[5]

---

[2] For more, see Anna-Maria Marshall, *Confronting Sexual Harassment: The Law and Politics of Everyday Life* (New York: Taylor & Francis Group, 2016), 22–25.

[3] Brittany Hoyos, "America's 'Best First Job'? My Story of Sexual Harassment at McDonald's," *The Guardian*, May 25, 2019.

[4] Ibid.

[5] Ibid.

Brittany Hoyos's story is not unique. Sexual harassment has been undermining the long-term earning capacity of women workers and contributing to the gender wage gap in the United States for as long as women have been working. According to the National Women's Law Center (NWLC), women make up nearly half of the workforce, yet "the conditions and practices they are routinely subjected to threaten their safety, their labor market participation, and their economic mobility and security."[6] Sexual harassment is not just about men behaving badly; it is a matter of economic security. Sexual harassment undercuts job performance and professional credibility. Those who keep their jobs may be obstructed in their careers by harassing supervisors or may decline opportunities for professional advancement in order to avoid the harassment. Women cannot "earn" their way out of harassment. Financial instability and fear of retaliation make it much more difficult for those being harassed to leave their place of employment or to advocate for meaningful change in the workplace. Fear of retaliation is greatest among low-wage workers like Hoyos, and the COVID-19 pandemic and ensuing financial crisis has only exacerbated the situation.[7] Additionally, sex and race discrimination often blend together in the workplace for women of color.[8] Immigrant and migrant workers face additional hurdles,

---

[6] Andrea Flynn, "Unsafe and Underpaid: How Sexual Harassment and Unfair Pay Hold Women Back," TIME'S UP Foundation (August 2020), 6.

[7] See Marion G. Crain and Kenneth Matheny, "Sexual Harassment and Solidarity," *George Washington Law Review* 87, no. 1 (2019): 76; Amanda Rossie, Jasmine Tucker, and Kayla Patrick, "Out of the Shadows: An Analysis of Sexual Harassment Charges Filed by Working Women," National Women's Law Center (2018), 9.

[8] For more, see Sandy Welsh, "Gender and Harassment," *Annual Review of Sociology* 25 (1999): 169–90 (at 170–76); and Maria L. Ontiveros, "Three Perspectives on Workplace Harassment of Women of Color," *Golden Gate University Law Review* 23, no. 3 (1993): 817–28.

such as language barriers and even the threat of deportation.[9] When women who are harassed do leave, they are more likely to take lower-paying jobs or exit the job market altogether. Sexual harassment has substantive long-term psychological and physical health ramifications.[10] Moreover, the majority of those harassed do not report incidents,[11] and women who stand up to their harassers are often punished for it; retaliation for reporting sexual harassment can result in further pay inequity. A recent report released by the NWLC revealed that 72 percent of workers who experienced sexual harassment faced retaliation for coming forward, including termination, poor performance evaluations, being sued for defamation, denial of promotions, and gaslighting.[12] Nearly one in five people reported that they were discouraged from pursuing legal action and/or explicitly told to keep the harassment quiet.[13] While people of all genders experience sexual harassment in the workplace, LGBTQ and BIPOC workers fare far worse than their white counterparts.[14] For example, while reports from white women workers have substantially declined in the past twenty years, the rate among African American workers has stayed consistent.[15]

---

[9] See Nichole Flores, "Trinity and Justice: A Theological Response to the Sexual Assault of Migrant Women," *Journal of Religion and Society* Supplement 16 (2018): 39–51.

[10] Rossie et al., "Out of the Shadows," 29.

[11] Carly McCann, Donald Tomaskovic-Devey, and M. V. Lee Badgett, "Employers' Responses to Sexual Harassment," *Center for Employment Equity* (December 1, 2018): 10.

[12] Jasmine Tucker and Jennifer Mondino, "Coming Forward: Key Trends and Data," National Women's Law Center (2020), 4.

[13] Ibid., 15.

[14] Ibid.

[15] Dan Cassino and Yasemin Besen-Cassino, "Race, Threat, and Workplace Sexual Harassment: The Dynamics of Harassment in the United States, 1997–2016," *Gender Work and Organization* 26 (2019): 1226–28. In 2016, African American women reported 3.8 times more incidents of sexual harassment than their white counterparts. Also see Rossie et al., "Out of the Shadows," 26.

While many Christian theologians, ministers, and scholars correctly interpret sexual harassment as a public health or civic issue, we struggle to understand stories like Brittany's as *our* moral problem. This is true even when sexual harassment and other forms of workplace violence are experienced and named as such by those among us whom we call friends and colleagues.[16] While it is tempting to suggest that the failure of theologians to address sexual violence is due to a lack of understanding, in the era of #MeToo, Title IX, and the Pennsylvania Grand Jury indictment,[17] this explanation feels "disingenuous, evasive, and simply inaccurate."[18] The problem cannot be that theologians, ministers, or scholars of religion fail to recognize rape, sexual harassment, or gender discrimination;[19] it is, rather, a failure to prioritize issues that do not directly have an impact on us, individually or collectively. Western culture is individualistic. Success is most often understood within a framework of *meritocracy,* the notion that my achievements are the result of my own individual hard work and effort. This is true even for professors of Christian theology and ethics because the university tenure and promotion system are based upon meritocracy. Within systems of meritocracy, people are trained to prioritize their own problems and self-interest, as everyone else is perceived as a potential competitor.

---

[16] For an example, see Donna Freitas, *Consent: A Memoir of Unwanted Attention* (New York: Little, Brown and Company, 2019).

[17] In 2018, a two-year Pennsylvania Grand Jury investigation revealed that more than three hundred Catholic priests across Pennsylvania sexually absued children and that the diocese covered it up. For more information, see Office of the Attorney General of the Commonwealth of Pennsylvania, "Pennsylvania Attorney General—Grand Jury Report," July 18, 2018.

[18] Karen Teel, "Can We Hear Him Now? James Cone's Enduring Challenge to White Theologians," *Theological Studies* 81, no. 3 (2020): 583. Here Teel makes a similar point with respect to whiteness.

[19] When I presented aspects of this chapter at the College Theology Society annual convention in 2019 to a room full of theologians, some were surprised by the high prevalence of sexual harassment. Still, no one contested the identification of Hoyos's story as sexual harassment.

This kind of individualist thinking then feeds into issues of justice and inequity. It is often more difficult for privileged people to address civic issues within their local communities. Problems that are external to our local community place less demand on us, financially and emotionally, as we do not perceive them as being direct competition for the same resources.

For many academics, Hoyos's experience of being sexually harassed while working an hourly-wage job to help her family pay the bills does not personally register within seminary or other educational structures. Instead, the topic of sexual violence remains at a distance, as something to study or write about. When sexual violence is addressed, it is often relegated to the realm of feminist or women's issues. In the classroom, at conferences, and in the larger society, many assume they already know enough and/or that the topic is irrelevant because they cannot imagine engaging in such egregious behavior themselves. Those without personal, lived experience of sexual trauma can read Hoyos's story and understand that what happened to her was wrong. But what if Hoyos was a student or employee at your school? What if Hoyos was a colleague in your division or a graduate student in your program? What if the person harassing her worked at your school? Would you believe her? Would you say something? What would you have to give up to do so? Advocating for people like Brittany Hoyos means going beyond "niceness."[20]

Educator Angelina Castagno defines niceness as "an embodied practice and a set of discursive expectations . . . that function as an institutional norm."[21] Niceness is not just tolerance; it encapsulates and connects things like white fragility, white saviors, and civility, in order to maintain inequity. Niceness captures how

---

[20] See Angelina Castagno, "Mapping the Contours of Niceness in Education," in *The Price of Nice: How Good Intentions Maintain Educational Inequity*, ed. Angelina Castagno (Minneapolis: University of Minnesota Press, 2019), xv.

[21] Ibid.

members of the dominant group use passive-aggressive behaviors to prevent those who are being discriminated against from speaking out. Niceness parades as "helping" behavior, making it very difficult to call out as a problem. For example, inviting the token person of color at work to happy hour, but ignoring the person once you are there. In this case, there is no concrete evidence of exclusion, but no one worked toward inclusion, either.

Castagno uses the category of niceness to address how racism and whiteness manifest at the micro level. For example, "nice people avoid potentially uncomfortable or upsetting experiences, knowledge and interactions."[22] Nice people do not create conflict or public disturbances. Niceness as a social construct avoids difficult conversations about race, advocates for colorblindness, and sees injustice as the result of the missteps of individuals. Niceness, Castagno writes, has a history that is rooted in "Black amiability and the 'slave's smile' . . . how femininity required Niceness while simultaneously constraining women's behavior and emotional life; and the contradicting images of American Niceness during the US occupation of the Philippines."[23] Nice people are not ignorant or unaware. Niceness is a white political and social construct that governs the rules of behavior, bodies, social interaction, and space.

White cis-male and cis-female theologians like to be nice. Niceness makes us feel good about ourselves. (After all, who wants to be considered mean?) It is much easier to protest and advocate for social change from a distance. In certain situations,

---

[22] Ibid., xx.

[23] Ibid., xvi. Controversy arose in the public sphere on how to reconcile US democratic sensibilities with imperialist desires at the turn of the twentieth century regarding the US occupation of the Philippines. As Carrie Tirado Bramen illustrates, mainstream news souces proliferated the notion that the United States governed through persuasion instead of brute force. See Carrie Tirado Bramen, *American Niceness: A Cultural History* (Cambridge, MA: Harvard University Press, 2017), chap. 5.

advocating for change at a distance is a prudent and necessary choice. Yet, I would like to suggest that it is also a privileged (read: white) choice. As argued previously, when it comes to matters of social transformation, justice cannot be "streamed on demand."[24] True crime serials and podcasts allow the viewer to engage real cases and social problems (such as sexual violence, homicide, racial profiling, and police corruption) from the comfort of their own homes, at a time of their convenience. While true crime media can be a good entry point for moral discussion and discernment, to stay in this fictitious space would be like living on television. Dominant strands of Catholic theology suffer from the same deficits of attention, wherein sexual violence remains a "women's issue" instead of an intersectional matter of practical consequence. It should be no surprise that young people turn elsewhere when looking for advice in matters of morals and relationships.[25]

Sexual violence, whether in the form of rape or sexual harassment, impacts real people. Sexual harassment is the most common way that people of all genders experience sexual violence, and it can have lasting economic and health consequences.[26] As a church, we need to start looking at what is going on behind the scenes. As activist theologian Robyn Henderson-Espinoza explains, there is a profound difference between theologies that develop in response to the "failings of the church" and those that arise in response to the "needs of the world."[27] In the former approach, the problem and its effects are defined by those "inside"

---

[24] Tanya Horeck, *Justice on Demand: True Crime in the Digital Streaming Era* (Detroit: Wayne State University Press, 2019), Kindle edition, 131.

[25] Notable exceptions exist, such as Margaret Farley, *Just Love: A Framework for Christian Sexual Ethics* (New York: Continuum, 2006).

[26] See E. G. Krug et al., eds., *World Report on Violence and Health* (Geneva: World Health Organization, 2002), 162–63.

[27] Robyn Henderson-Espinoza, *Activist Theology* (Minneapolis: Fortress Press, 2019), 71.

the institution (i.e., people who feel comfortable speaking out and who already have a place at the table). The latter approach widens the net and looks to define both the problem and solution by bringing in perspectives from outside of the church from the start. As scholars and educators, we cannot expect our students or congregations to take us seriously if we do not have our own house in order. The reluctance of religious and theological communities to adequately address matters of sexual injustice among us represents a profound failure of moral imagination.[28] In what follows, I address sexual harassment because it is the most commonly experienced form of sexual violence. It is also not taken seriously.

WHAT IS SEXUAL HARASSMENT?

Sexual harassment is illegal because it is a form of discrimination. "Sexual harassment constitutes discrimination because it is harmful and it is based on gender."[29] Traditionally, two categories have been used to describe experiences of harassment: quid pro quo and hostile work environment. More recently, however, legal scholars and the social sciences have recognized that biological sex and gender socialization intersect with a person's gender. Gender is a social and legal category that extends beyond the labels of male or female. It is often confused with biological sex, which is based upon chromosomes. Most people express their gender identity as masculine or feminine. When a person's gender identity matches their biological sex, they are

---

[28] Megan McCabe makes a similar point with respect to rape culture in "A Feminist Catholic Response to the Social Sin of Rape Culture," *Journal of Religious Ethics* 46 no. 4 (2018): 635–57.

[29] Frazier F. Benya, Paula A. Johnson, and Sheila E. Widnall, eds., *Sexual Harassment of Women: Climate, Culture, and Consequences in Academic Sciences, Engineering, and Medicine* (Washington, DC: The National Academies Press, 2018), 25. Sexual harassment is derived from Title IX, which does not allow discrimination on the basis of gender.

called cisgender. Other people (transgender people) feel that their assigned gender does not match how they feel inside. It is important to remember that everyone is different.[30] Sexual harassment applies in all gendered contexts. Moreover, as sexual harassment is not necessarily motivated by sexual desire, and doesn't always involve sexual activity, most find it more accurate to use the following three categories: sexual coercion, unwanted sexual attention, and gender harassment.

- *Sexual coercion* is quid pro quo sexual harassment. In this case, acceptance of or collaboration with sexual advances becomes conditional for employment or education.

- *Unwanted sexual attention* refers to sexual advances that are not reciprocated and offensive to the target, such as touching, hugging, stroking, or persistent requests for dates despite discouragement. Unwanted sexual attention can also include assault. Unlike sexual coercion, no conditions are attached for employment or educational advancement.

- *Gender harassment,* as defined by psychologists Louise Fitzgerald, Michele Gelfand, and Fritz Drasgow, can be understood as "a broad range of verbal and nonverbal behaviors not aimed at sexual cooperation, but that convey insulting, hostile, and degrading attitudes about members of one gender."[31] Gender harassment is the most common form of sexual harassment. Examples include telling women to shut up, name calling, demeaning jokes, sabotaging behaviors, or making comments expressing that women do not belong in places of leadership. These same kinds of gender harassment also apply to men who do not exhibit

---

[30] For more information, visit "Coming Out," a resource of the Human Rights Campaign. Faith-based resources include New Ways Ministry and Religious Institute.

[31] Louise F. Fitzgerald, Michele J. Gelfand, and Fritz Drasgow, "Measuring Sexual Harassment: Theoretical and Psychometric Advances," *Basic and Applied Social Psychology* 17, no. 4 (1995): 430.

traditionally masculine attributes, and to sexual minorities such as gay men and bisexual women.

Yet even these traditional categories remain limited, as they struggle to account for the ways in which sexual harassment intersects with other forms of workplace discrimination.[32]

Sexual harassment can also be ambient, in that it is "not targeted at any specific individual or group of individuals."[33] Common examples of ambient sexual harassment include the posting of pornographic imagery in a common area in a workplace or the use of sexually abusive language in a public educational setting or workspace. Scholars have likened the effects of ambient sexual harassment to that of secondhand smoke.

Environments that have historically had higher rates of sexual harassment share the following characteristics: (1) there is a high perceived tolerance of (or indifference to) sexual harassment; (2) leadership is male dominated, and the power is hierarchal with strong dependencies on those at higher levels; and (3) people are geographically isolated. To be very clear, I am not suggesting that all men in leadership sexually harass their employees. However, such environments are less likely to have taken serious measures to address sexual harassment.[34]

Adequately addressing sexual harassment requires changing the culture of an organization. To do this, "it is crucial to recognize that organizational cultures are not neutral."[35] Instead, they reflect the values and norms of those who have been and are in roles of leadership, the norms of formal and informal structures, and the sociocultural situation in which institutions are situated. In particular, norms surrounding "where women belong and *which* women

---

[32] Benya et al, *Sexual Harassment of Women*, 24.

[33] Kristin H. Berger Parker, "Ambient Harassment under Title VII: Reconsidering the Workplace Environment," *Northwestern University Law Review* 102, no. 2 (2008): 947.

[34] See Benya et al., *Sexual Harassment of Women*, 16.

[35] Ibid., 123.

belong where" are a key driver of structural injustice.[36] Religion plays a key role in shaping these norms, including in the culture of theological studies and pastoral workplaces in the United States.

For centuries, dominant strands within the Christian tradition have regarded women as incompetent, less holy, and unfit for leadership within the public domain.[37] For example, Augustine believed that women were spiritually equal to men but inferior when it comes to matters of embodiment.[38] He concedes that women are redeemable, but are more prone to sin without her male counterpart.[39] Thomas Aquinas accepts Aristotelian categories and understands women "as less rational than men."[40] While Augustine and Aquinas lived centuries ago, the doctrines and practices of many Catholic Christian traditions remain influenced by them.[41] In particular, the idea that women are less rational, and subsequently, incapable of making sound moral judgments lingers in cultures marked by clericalism.[42] Today,

---

[36] Flynn, "Unsafe and Underpaid," 14.

[37] Much of this attitude arises out of a theological anthropology marked by neo-Platonic dualisms of mind over body, and objectivity over subjectivity, which have supported male hegemony within the Christian tradition. It is worth noting that these same dualisms are also linked to racist and anti-Semitic claims. Elena Procario-Foley makes this point in "Liberating Jesus: Christian Feminism and Anti-Judaism," in *Frontiers in Catholic Feminist Theology: Shoulder to Shoulder*, ed. Susan Abraham and Elena Procario-Foley (Minneapolis: Fortress Press, 2009), 108–10. Also see Kelly Brown Douglas, *What's Faith Got to Do with It? Black Bodies/Christian Souls* (Maryknoll, NY: Orbis Books, 2005), 42–53.

[38] Augustine, *De Trinitate* 12.7.10.

[39] Ibid., 7.7.10.

[40] See Lisa Sowle Cahill, "Catholic Feminists and Traditions: Renewal, Reinvention, Replacement," *Journal of the Society of Christian Ethics* 34, no. 2 (2014): 33.

[41] While this may not have been Augustine's intention, his interpretation of original sin continues to shape Western notions of sexuality and gender. See Elaine Pagels, *Adam, Eve, and the Serpent* (New York: Vintage Books, 1988).

[42] Clericalism is an attitude or expectation that ordained ministers are morally superior to all others. Lay people can foster clericalism through excessive deference to ministers.

the majority of professionally educated lay ministers employed in Roman Catholic parishes in the United States are women. Yet, the decisions continue to be made by male leaders at the diocesan and parish level. Those who teach seminarians (future priests) in the Roman Catholic Church are also predominantly male theologians.[43]

THEOLOGICAL ROOTS OF (DIS)BELIEF

In May 2020, news reports broke of allegations of sexual abuse against liturgical composer David Haas. Since then, an additional forty-four women have come forward, reporting sexually abusive conduct by Haas between 1979 and 2019. While Haas initially denied the allegations, several months later he issued an apology for the harm he had caused.[44] Despite recent acknowledgments of the role of clericalism by Pope Francis and many contemporary theologians, there remains little conversation about more systematic patterns of abuse and its theological roots. In an op-ed published by the *National Catholic Reporter* in the summer of 2020, shortly after allegations against Haas first surfaced, Jamie Manson wrote: "Part of the doubt cast on Haas' victims is rooted in our theological tradition that trains us to not believe women."[45] Yet, the Roman Catholic theological tradition is also

---

[43] David DeLamb, *Lay Parish Ministers* (New York: National Pastoral Life Center, 2005). An estimated 80 percent of those working in paid positions in the church are women (the closing of the National Pastoral Life Center in 2009 has made it difficult to collect more recent data). Also see Susan Ross, "Feminist Theology and the Clergy Sexual Abuse Crisis," *Theological Studies* 80, no. 3 (2019): 638n29.

[44] "'Statement Regarding David Haas' by Bishop James P. Powers," *Catholic Herald*, October 30, 2020. See also Maria Wiering, "Catholic Composer Denies Claims of Sexual Misconduct; Publisher Cuts Ties," *Crux*, June 18, 2020.

[45] Jamie Manson is the first person I have seen who has substantively made this connection in print. See "We Need to Talk about David Haas," *National Catholic Reporter*, June 30, 2020.

racialized in ways that render white women's suffering culturally intelligible, but not BIPOC women's suffering. In what follows, I briefly examine key factors in Roman Catholicism that have shaped the theological roots of a culture of disbelief: gender complementarity, the centering of male holiness, and white entitlement. I address these separately and together as they inform cultural ideologies and practices surrounding sexual violence. However, in Western culture, they interact to form "a matrix of problems" for women in ministry and beyond.[46]

GENDER COMPLEMENTARITY AND "HIMPATHY"

Catholic theological anthropology is rooted in notions of gender complementarity. This means that women and men have distinct roles and inclinations in church, society, and family that are revealed by sexual anatomy. Specifically, women and men are created in God's image *"to an equal degree,"* and "they are also called *to exist mutually 'one for the other.'"*[47] This sets in motion a relational ontology in which masculinity and femininity define one another by means of exclusion (John Paul II uses the language of *"complete and explain each other"*).[48] In this framework, God created men to take initiative (lead) at home and in society and women to be receptive to men's initiative (obey, follow) and serve.[49] In the context of the doctrinal history of the Roman Catholic Church, these norms have been used to justify the exclusion of women from decision-making and leadership roles

---

[46] Emilie M. Townes, "Lament and Hope: Defying This Hot Mess," *Reflections: Yale Divinity School* (Fall 2019): 40.

[47] John Paul II, *Mulieris Dignitatem: On the Dignity and Vocation of Women on the Occasion of the Marian Year* (August 12, 1988), nos. 6, 7.

[48] Ibid., no. 25.

[49] For example, see Sacred Congregation for the Doctrine of the Faith, *Inter Insigniores: On the Question of Admission of Women to the Ministerial Priesthood* (October 15, 1978); and *Mulieris Dignitatem,* no. 10.

in public life.[50] For example, while more women participate in lay ministry, they do not hold managerial positions, and they do not experience their ideas as being taken seriously. Only recently have women been invited to participate in senior roles in the Vatican.

This is only part of the story when it comes to matters of sexual violence. As Jamie Manson explains: "When religious power is totally in the hands of men, it creates a culture of devaluation and distrust of women. Men support one another and cover for one another, and they treat women as disposable and their stories unworthy of belief. Rather than listen to survivors, we silence them or blame them for leading men into temptation."[51] At stake is a culture of disbelief and silence. My students who participate in athletics and Greek life understand this in terms of not wanting to "rat out" a team member or sorority member. While all social groups have codes for membership, in Roman Catholicism sexual abuse cannot be separated from male-female gender complementarity because the "rules" for membership are embedded within a climate of what writer Kate Manne terms *himpathy*.[52] (To be clear, the "rules" to which I refer are not literal, nor are they spoken out loud. They are implicit community norms.)

"Himpathy" is a racist heteropatriarchal form of empathy, wherein excessive sympathy flows toward white, middle-class, able-bodied men because of how they look and where they are socially positioned in society.[53] Moreover, as Manne illustrates, the excessive sympathy that flows to privileged white men *who*

---

[50] For example, see Bishops' Committee on Women in Society and in the Church, *Consultation with Women in Diocesan Leadership* (Washington, DC: USCCB, October 2001).

[51] Manson, "We Need to Talk about David Haas."

[52] "Himpathy" is Kate Manne's term. See *Down Girl: The Logic of Misogyny* (New York: Oxford University Press, 2017), 23ff., 179, 197.

[53] Ibid., 201.

commit assaults "contributes to insufficient concern for the harm, humiliation, and (more or less lasting) trauma that they may bring to their victims."[54] In the case of male dominance, himpathy often works to make the male who committed the assault appear to be the "victim." Manne uses the example of Stanford swimmer Brock Turner, who raped a twenty-two-year-old woman behind a dumpster and left her there, unconscious.[55] As Manne notes, the judge in this case was more concerned about the "severe impact" of sentencing on Turner's future athletic career than about what had happened to the survivor.[56] But in this instance, it wasn't just the judge or Turner's father who expressed "excessive sympathy"; women did as well, writing character references and remaining silent.[57] Himpathy primes the situation for victim blaming by "[failing] to question the collective presumption that [the accused male] is trustworthy."[58] As Manne explains, in "'her word against his' scenarios, we move from the premise that he's an 'honorable man' or 'good guy' to the conclusions that she must be lying or hysterical."[59] This is even in the face of scientific evidence to the contrary.

In religious contexts, himpathy is further exacerbated by clericalism and patriarchal interpretations of the doctrine of God. Within the Christian West, dominant voices emphasized the maleness of Jesus in the incarnation of God. For example, as feminist theologian Susan Ross states, "The argument of *Inter Insigniores* (1976) is that not only was the intention of Christ and of the early church to establish a male-only priesthood, but

---

[54] Ibid.

[55] Ibid., 196. For a description of the case, see Liam Stack, "In Stanford Rape Case, Brock Turner Blamed Drinking and Promiscuity," *New York Times*, June 8, 2016.

[56] Manne, *Down Girl*, 197.

[57] Lily Herman, "The Stanford Rapist's Supporters Have Just Apologized for Defending Him," *Teen Vogue*, June 9, 2016.

[58] Manne, *Down Girl*, 180.

[59] Ibid.

also that ordaining women would not only violate the 'natural resemblance' needed to see Christ in the priest, but also the spousal identity of the church."[60] Male and female theologians have critiqued this argument on the grounds that the tradition and relevant biblical passages should be interpreted within historical context.[61] This, along with a gendered ecclesiological framework marked by feminine (lay) obedience to masculine (clerical) leadership, is particularly difficult to uproot because of how Catholics have been socialized. As Ross notes:

> It is surely the case that not every priest or lay person has understood the identification of the priest with the divine in a literal sense. The sacrality attached to the priest, however, has been understood not only as a theological reality, but a personal one as well. Many can recall being taught that a priest's hands were especially sacred, and that the sacrament of holy orders had produced an ontological change in the priest, raising him above the laity. The priest occupied a place in the church and in the imagination of the people as the earthly representation of the divine, and lay people were socialized in obedience to this representative.[62]

Her point is that religious people have been socialized to see priests, and sometimes even men in general, as embodying and enfleshing the divine. When it comes to himpathy, this means that a religious person has to overcome not only sociocultural gendered and racial norms regarding authority and credibility, but also must come face to face with deep-seated beliefs about

---

[60] Ross, "Feminist Theology and the Clergy Sexual Abuse Crisis," 638.

[61] See for example, Elisabeth Schüssler Fiorenza, *A Discipleship of Equals: A Critical Feminist Ekklesia-ology of Liberation* (New York: Herder and Herder, 1993); and Gary Macy, *The Hidden History of Women's Ordination: Female Clergy in the Medieval West* (Oxford University Press, 2008).

[62] Ross, "Feminist Theology and the Clergy Sexual Abuse Crisis," 637–38.

who God is and how God is manifest here on earth. This is very difficult for most Christians, given the emphasis placed on Jesus's maleness. As a result, it can be much easier psychologically, socially, and theologically to blame the victims of clerical abuse rather than the abusers themselves. This is why, despite knowing of a serious claim of sexual assault against Haas, the Archdiocese of St. Paul and Minneapolis allowed him to continue working with teenagers. It is also why many who come forward to tell their stories are blamed and harassed on social media, and why some choose not to tell their stories for fear of such online harassment. I experienced this firsthand when I worked as a pastoral minister and witnessed a male colleague engage in inappropriate behavior on a youth ministry retreat. I reported the incident and the parish investigated, but as the young women involved did not report the incident, and in the absence of others who could corroborate my statement, the parish was unable to address the issue.

When it comes to the workplace, male-female gender complementarity makes it all too easy to dismiss the significance of harassment in the first place, such as by providing justification for why women do not belong at work to begin with because they create distractions or are not tough enough to handle it. Yet, himpathy is only the tip of the iceberg: "We should also be concerned with the rewarding and valorizing of women who conform to gendered norms and expectations, enforce the 'good' behavior of others and engage in certain forms of patriarchal virtue signaling, . . . slut shaming, victim blaming."[63] Toward this end, I think it is particularly helpful to return to Castagno's notion of niceness. American niceness is rooted in the basic assumption that "Americans are decent and good-natured people with the best of intentions."[64] When Americans do something damaging, it is much more likely to be passed off as a mistake.

---

[63] Manne, *Down Girl*, 192.
[64] Castagno, "Mapping the Contours," xiii.

The concept of niceness is often applied to white women, especially those who adopt traditional notions of gender.[65] Nice white women are docile and subservient to white men. Nice white women do not challenge white men. They sympathize with white men. Women who do not contest traditional notions of male-female gender complementarity are nice white women. In this way, *male-female gender complementarity* is a racialized construct centered on white entitlement.

WHITE ENTITLEMENT

When I assign the work of James Cone or M. Shawn Copeland, many of my white students resist learning on the grounds that they cannot relate to the material. This reaction surprises me, in part because many of the same students support the #BlackLivesMatter movement. While their reaction to Cone and Copeland likely reflects a range of experiences (e.g., the classroom environment, peer pressure, and family histories), notions of white goodness or white entitlement are in the backdrop. In *Knowing Christ Crucified: The Witness of African American Religious Experience,* womanist theologian M. Shawn Copeland foregrounds the issues of selective memory and intentional forgetting within Roman Catholicism. She stresses that "memory can fade, may be altered or manipulated," but forgetting "includes both unintentional failures to notice something or someone and intentional acts of erasure or deletion of what once was known."[66] Forgetting the plantation, which Copeland names as "the Golgotha of Black experience in the

---

[65] See Sally Campbell Galman, "Nice Work: Young White Women, Near Enemies, and Teaching inside the Magic Circle," in Castagno, *The Price of Nice*, 70–90.

[66] M. Shawn Copeland, *Knowing Christ Crucified: The Witness of African American Religious Experience* (Maryknoll, NY: Orbis Books, 2018), 95–96.

United States," is an institutional failure and erasure as much as it is an individual one.[67] Or as philosopher Shannon Sullivan suggests, "A great deal of [white domination] functions through the practices and habits of individual white people and the predominantly white families and communities to which they belong."[68] White people are responsible for white supremacy because our actions and beliefs contribute to systems that make up the world in which we live. The two cannot be easily separated; the political is personal.

It took me a long time to realize that "I can't learn this because I can't relate to it" is a way of avoiding interpersonal and internal conflict. For white people, figuring out how to situate ourselves imaginatively in relation to chattel slavery means rejecting narratives of white moral goodness. This requires the kind of moral imagination that many white people have yet to explore. For white peope who see themselves as "good" (read: nice) or those who "consider themselves to be non- or anti-racist," this is particularly challenging work because they think they know what to do.[69] Or, at least they think they know what *not* to do. This makes it really hard for them to detect and challenge their own racial biases. For example, "good" white mothers ensure that their children have access to high-quality educational opportunities. In most areas of the United States, this means you have to live in a white neighborhood and send your child to private or charter schools. This increases the likelihood that their children will receive a whitewashed education. "Good" white mothers ensure that their children have access to premium groceries (read: organic). They do not let their children live in conditions marked by utter filth.[70]

---

[67] Ibid., 125.

[68] Shannon Sullivan, *Good White People: The Problem with Middle-Class White Anti-Racism* (Albany: SUNY Press, 2014), Kindle edition, 2.

[69] Ibid., 5.

[70] Ibid., 89–91.

Through social interactions and white parenting, white children learn how to be white.[71]

In *They Were Her Property: White Women as Slave Owners in the American South*, historian Stephanie Jones-Rogers describes the experiences of formerly enslaved persons with white female slave owners. White young women were gifted enslaved persons as Christmas and wedding gifts. "Elite members of the planter class presented their children with enslaved people at elaborate events following their wedding processions."[72] When Mary Homer married William Johnson, her father presented her with fifty enslaved persons at a great ceremony. This was often done as a part of women's coming of age. Enslaved persons were sold to finance weddings, to purchase dresses, and the like.[73] Young women were taught how to "manage" a household, which included disciplining enslaved persons. As such, chattel slavery cannot be separated from white women's gender socialization. Moreover, owning a person was a mark of status, just as much for white men as it was for white women. Within this context, white men believed they were entitled to rape enslaved women. As Kelly Brown Douglas illustrates, myths about Black women as lewd, lascivious, tempting, and sexually insatiable were used to justify sexual relations between enslaved women and slave owners. Furthermore, within the institution of chattel slavery, enslaved persons were considered property, so they could not legally be raped.[74] White

---

[71] There are a number of excellent books on this topic. See, e.g., Beverly Tatum, *Why Are All the Black Kids Sitting Together in the Cafeteria? And Other Conversations about Race,* rev. ed. (New York: Basic Books, 2017); and Margaret Hagarmen, *White Kids: Growing Up with Privilege in a Racially Divided America* (New York: NYU Press, 2018).

[72] Stephanie E. Jones-Rogers, *They Were Her Property: White Women as Slave Owners in the American South* (New Haven, CT: Yale University Press, 2019), Kindle edition, 18.

[73] Ibid., 18, 142.

[74] See Kelly Brown Douglas, *Stand Your Ground: Black Bodies and the Justice of God* (Maryknoll, NY: Orbis Books, 2015), especially 64–68.

women were not passive bystanders in this context. They knew their fathers, brothers, sons, and husbands were raping enslaved women. In some cases, white women were jealous. One formerly enslaved woman recounts being sold twice; the first time was because she resisted the sexual advances of her mistress's son, and the second time was because her pale skin was perceived as threatening.[75] As Jones-Rogers illustrates, these actions concretely demonstrate that white women of the house knew that Black enslaved women were being raped. "These white women did not sell enslaved people out of necessity; they got rid of them because of shame, jealousy, and anger."[76]

In this way, tolerating sexual violence against Black and Indigenous women has been embedded in the gendered identity of white women for centuries. In the case of African slaves, white men claimed they owned the bodies of the African women that they raped and trafficked. Christianity was used by white male and female perpetrators of violence to justify their brutality at the pulpit and in the home. Neither love of neighbor, nor solidarity with the poor, nor human dignity, nor justice lays claim to the moral integrity of white Christian women in the way that whiteness does.[77]

Reckoning with this history is not easy. The primary goal for religious people in the context of sexual violence, in particular for white Christian women, cannot be "breaking the silence."[78] This is because the fundamental moral problem is not lack of awareness. In all of the instances discussed in this chapter, the moral problem is not a failure to recognize that sexual violation has occurred. In each instance, someone explicitly knew that the rape, harassment, or assault happened. In the Haas case, the arch-

---

[75] Jones-Rodgers, *They Were Her Property*, 22, 143.

[76] Ibid., 143.

[77] Ibid., 6.

[78] Traci C. West, *Solidarity and Defiant Spirituality: Africana Lessons on Religion, Racism, and Ending Gender Violence* (New York: NYU Press, 2019), 46.

diocese knew about his sexually explicit behavior with a minor. In the context of chattel slavery, children and pregnancy on the plantation were the most basic evidence of rape. White mistresses were threatened by enslaved women with lighter skin pigmentation. Records and oral histories show that formerly enslaved women with lighter melanin were sold not out of necessity but out of jealousy, anger, and shame.[79] Similarly, fellow employees witnessed and participated in Brittany Hoyos's harassment. Upper management knew what happened to Brittany Hoyos because she told them about it.

Across the nation, colleges and universities engage in awareness campaigns. October is domestic-violence-awareness month; April is sexual-assault-awareness month; March is for women's history; February is for Black history; and the list goes on. Awareness is important. Yet, awareness is inadequate as a moral aim because it assumes that knowledge is enough of a motivating factor to encourage, empower, and embolden nice people to act. Or rather, it supports the counterclaim, which is that mistreatment of people is the result of ignorance. Throughout history knowledge of wrongdoing has never been enough to stop entire groups of people who benefit from the subjugation of others. We have to go deeper and ask: *What does tolerating sexual violence protect? Whom does it benefit?*

Niceness serves the dominant group. This is even the case in religiously affiliated institutions that have a call to justice and service in the world. In such contexts, failure to take all forms of sexual violence, including sexual harassment, seriously turns one's efforts to embody the institution's mission into an exercise in self-denigration and self-deletion, as participation can mean putting up with self-erasure. Within religious contexts, this erasure is multiplied as it sends a message to the broader community that ignoring and tolerating gender-based violence and harassment

---

[79] Jones-Rogers, *They Were Her Property*, 143.

is in keeping with a divinely ordained structure marked by sacrificial suffering and male headship.[80]

To be clear, the kind of erasure I am speaking of is not only literal; nor is it symbolic; it is pragmatic. Philosopher Sara Ahmed illustrates this by referring to a family gathering "having polite conversations, where only certain things can be brought up."[81] In this context, the person who exposes the problem is usually heard as the cause of the problem insofar as "she stops the smooth flow of communication. It becomes tense. She makes things tense."[82] The issue is not so much about what is being said, or even how it is being said. Instead, "[the person] is getting in the way of something, the achievement or accomplishment of the family or of some *we* or other, which is created by what is not said."[83] Note the deletion or silence occurs in an effort to preserve something else. The woman in Ahmed's narrative is a problem not because of the content of her speech or even because of the discomfort her speaking causes. She is a problem because she is getting in the way of another's accomplishment. This explains why some cases of sexual harassment and sexual violence are addressed and others are not. The more a case gets in the way of someone else's accomplishment, the more likely the victim-survivor is to be ignored, blamed, shamed, or silenced.

It might look something like this: A woman submits a complaint to human resources regarding bullying, racism, and misogyny in her department. She collects the testimonies of twenty people. When she submits the material to human resources, she is told that she has a "chip on her shoulder." As Ahmed notes, "It is as if she put a complaint forward as a way of putting herself

---

[80] One of the more contentious places that this plays out is the doctrine of atonement. See Chapter 7 for a discussion.

[81] Sara Ahmed, *Living a Feminist Life* (Durham, NC: Duke University Press, 2017), 37.

[82] Ibid.

[83] Ibid.

forward; a complaint is often treated as self-promotional."[84] Another scenario could be this: A woman of color has a meeting with a friend who has just become the new dean of the college. The new dean refers to a "difficult history" between the woman and a former department head and says, "I want you to reconcile with him, because all he did was write you some nasty emails."[85] In each case the harassment is minimized and explained away, and there is an effort to discredit the character of the one who has experienced the harassment, thus preserving the comfort and stature of an invisible "we" (the dominant culture). In this way, the silence, erasure, and ignoring rewards the behavior, values, and ideals of the dominant culture or group.

Taking a cue from Ahmed, theological and religious institutions need to ask themselves: What is the accomplishment, goal, or achievement that giving due attention to sexual violence disrupts? What is the invisible "we" that her speaking, his speaking, or their speaking out disturbs?[86] In many cases, it is white women and white men who benefit most from the culture of misogyny. I know that women are an easy target when it comes to sexual violence. Having worked with many women who are survivors and as a survivor myself, I understand this on a deeply personal level. This is really hard—I get it. Yet, white women have not been there for BIPOC colleagues, in the past or in the present. This may have been because white women are still trying to understand how whiteness works. Or it may have been because we were caught in the dynamics of niceness. We were too worried about our own inclusion, success, failures, and suffering to notice those around us. We were caught up in being nice. But "nice" is a low bar for moral behavior.

---

[84] Summarized and slightly adapted from Sara Ahmed, "White Friend," *Feminist Killjoys,* blog, May 31, 2019.

[85] Ibid.

[86] Adapted from Ahmed, *Living a Feminist Life,* 37.

While the majority of management positions in the United States continue to be held by white men, white women benefit from the privilege that comes from being less different than people of color are from white men.[87] Even when we are not directly in positions of power, white women can use our access to those in dominant positions to exert influence. Examples of this can range from networking opportunities, funding, increased responsibility at work, and the opportunity to do one's own scholarship on feminism with few consequences. Too many white women (as well as women of color) know what it is like to be passed over for leadership opportunitities, only to be later told that something is inherently wrong with them precisely because they do not have enough leadership experience. This is not acceptable. At the same time, it is important to point out that whiteness, class, ability, and access to education are what make our participation possible in the first place.

To give you a personal example, as a white feminist scholar at a Catholic, predominantly white institution in the Northeast, my whiteness outweighs my gender within the intricate system of costs and rewards. While I have experienced personal costs because my scholarship is not neutral on matters of gender or race, I am not expected to speak for all women in the workplace. In fact, my whiteness gives me the *option* of remaining silent when it comes to matters of racial and gender injustice. I have this option because other white women in my workplace care about the same issues I do. I also have this option because most administrators are white. But even if my integrity does not allow me to ignore justice issues within the public sphere, I am not being watched to the same degree as my BIPOC colleagues.

---

[87] In 2019, women held 32.3 percent of all management positions. Of those positions, Latinas held 4.3 percent, Black women 4 percent, and Asian American women 2.5 percent. Catalyst, *Quick Take: Women in Management* (August 11, 2020).

There is no expectation that I will represent my race when I walk into the classroom or faculty meeting. To put it bluntly, white women can choose to give attention to matters of injustice at a time that is convenient for them. (It is worth noting that white men participate in this dynamic as well.) White women who play the game—who don't "rock the boat," so to speak—are rewarded. But those who transgress the unspoken rules and call out white entitlement are made aware of the costs of membership in the white majority—they must toe the line, or they will be marginalized.

White feminist theologians, myself included, have given scant attention to the rape of Indigenous, Black, migrant, Latinx, and Asian American women. When we do talk about rape or other forms of sexual violence, race and ethnicity tend to fall out of the picture. To date, white Christian feminist theological discourse has yet to take substantive and sustained account of the role of whiteness in rape culture. Even though white feminist theologians cite the work of BIPOC scholars and frame sexual violence in intersectional terms, rarely is it the case that we substantively engage our own whiteness.

When feminist work, theological or otherwise, attends to sexual violence without critical engagement of institutional power, it reinforces whiteness. This is because to understand the state, the police, or governing bodies as protective or neutral is a function of white entitlement.[88] Therefore, feminist theological discourse on sexual violence must do more than engage diverse voices. We must explicitly engage matters of criminal justice and white-collar crime within the very spaces that we inhabit. We must ask, for example, what are the behaviors of "good" white women in the academy? At church? In the community? How are those behaviors rewarded?

---

[88] Katti Gray, "'Invisible No More:' The Other Women #MeToo Should Defend," *The Crime Report*, January 30, 2018.

BLESSED ARE THOSE WHO BELIEVE[89]

At the beginning of Luke's Gospel, we learn that Mary, who is from an "insignificant town, is to marry a man from the line of David."[90] The reader finds a young child, pregnant and from a lower class, who is to marry into a royal lineage. You can only imagine the gossip. Mary heads out to visit a priest and his wife in the hill country. The class differences between Elizabeth and Mary would have been stark.[91] When Mary arrives, Elizabeth, advanced in age, says:

> "Blessed are you among women, and blessed is the fruit of your womb. And why has this happened to me, that the mother of my Lord comes to me? For as soon as I heard the sound of your greeting, the child in my womb leaped for joy" (Lk 1:42-44).

Feminist scholars have emphasized the prophetic nature of Elizabeth's speaking.[92] Biblical scholar Jean-Pierre Ruiz points out that redactional studies of Luke 1:39–56 suggest that verses 46–56 (often termed Mary's canticle) were added at a later moment of composition, thus making unclear who mentors whom in the text.[93] Therefore, a deeper investigation of what Elizabeth

---

[89] This musing is inspired by the methodology present in Valdir Steuernagel, "Doing Theology Together with Mary," *Journal of Latin American Theology* 8, no. 2 (2013): 9–49.

[90] Stephanie Buckhanon Crowder, *When Momma Speaks: The Bible through African American Motherhood* (Louisville, KY: WJK Press, 2016), 76.

[91] Ibid., 75–76. Elizabeth was a member of the daughters of Aaron, a priestly line. See Loretta Dornish, *A Woman Reads the Gospel of Luke* (Collegeville, MN: Liturgical Press, 1996), 13.

[92] There are many examples. Elizabeth A. Johnson gives a good summary of the literature in *Truly Our Sister: A Theology of Mary in the Communion of Saints* (New York: Continuum, 2006), 258–74.

[93] Jean-Pierre Ruiz, "Luke 1:39–56: Mary's Visit to Elizabeth as Biblical Instance of Mentoring," *Apuntes* 17, no. 4 (Winter 1997): 103.

means when she wonders, "Why has this happened to me?" is important.[94] While surprise, joy, and astonishment are all possibilities, given the context of the biblical passage, serious consideration of the social differences between Elizabeth and Mary makes disdain equally plausible. I have always thought it highly likely that aristocratic, pregnant Elizabeth might not have been entirely pleased to find an unwed, pregnant child at her doorstep. Perhaps, due in part to the desire not to look like an idiot, and in part to God's grace, she finds a way to deal with the situation. At least, it's worth pondering this as a possibility.

But what happens next is really interesting: Elizabeth "attentively listens to Mary's greeting that sets off the unborn John the Baptist's joyful leap, and Elizabeth herself utters a blessing that underlines the close connection between faith and attention to God's word."[95] In Luke 1:45, we read: "Blessed is she who believed that there would be a fulfillment of what was spoken to her by the Lord." Elizabeth decides to believe Mary, and their common ground is empowering. Elizabeth does not ask Mary about the circumstances of her pregnancy; she does not ask for details of how she became pregnant, or for proof that the child is Joseph's. Believing and blessing are not compatible with belittling, infantilizing, or questioning credibility. Believing and blessing are empowering actions grounded in the concreteness of daily life. And in this case, believing was supported by Zechariah, Elizabeth's husband. Women's relationships must be supported by the men around them, and Elizabeth does not stay at Mary's side forever. Mary moves on without her, with a role in God's "kin-dom" far surpassing Elizabeth's.

---

[94] Ruiz suggests that the text is not entirely clear on the meaning of this phrase. See ibid., 104.

[95] Ibid.

5

RACIAL INJUSTICE AND TRUE CRIME

"Whatever you do for me, without me, you do to me."
—MR. R, CRIMINAL (IN)JUSTICE PODCAST

On April 19, 1989, Trisha Meili was assaulted and raped in New York City's Central Park when she went out for an evening jog. She was raped, severely beaten, dragged off the path, and left for dead. Four hours later, when a passerby found Meili, her body temperature had fallen to 84 degrees Fahrenheit and she had lost 75 percent of her blood. That same evening, a group of about thirty young Black and Latino/as had gathered in another area of the park. The police were called to investigate several minor incidents that occurred in the park that evening, such as badgering a homeless man for food, intimidating bike riders, and harassing a man at the reservoir.[1] Over the next several hours, several Black and Latino boys were taken in for questioning in conjunction with the Meili case. They were threatened and deprived of food and sleep, and some were

---

[1] Jim Dwyer, "The True Story of How a City in Fear Brutalized the Central Park Five," *New York Times*, May 30, 2019.

questioned without their parents present. Some of the inter-
rogations lasted up to twenty-eight hours. While they did not
confess to raping Meili, they did implicate each other and
confessed to hitting or holding her.[2] Even though the DNA
evidence did not connect any of these young men to the assault, public opinion condemned them in the media.

In the two weeks following the attack, the case was covered 406
times in New York's four daily newspapers and six broadcast news
stations. Race was mentioned as a possible explanation for the
crime twice as often as any other factor.[3] Yusef Salaam, Korey Wise,
Kevin Richardson, Raymond Santana, and Antron McCray were
described "using emotional negative language 390 times, including 185 animal images such as 'wolves,' 'pack,' and 'herd.'"[4] Instead
of relying upon appropriate legal terms to describe the case (i.e.,
rape, assault, battery), "the media relied on the word 'wilding' for
purposes of news sensationalism."[5] Through its repeated use, the
term amplified public fears of violence and came to signify a form
of lawlessness predominantly associated with sexual violence and
savagery, committed by groups of young Black and Latino men.[6]

---

[2] Sarah Burns, *The Central Park Five: A Chronicle of a City Wilding* (New York: Alfred A. Knopf, 2011), 20–31; Greg Stratton, "Transforming the Central Park Jogger into the Central Park Five: Shifting Narratives of Innocence and Changing Media Discourse in the Attack on the Central Park Jogger, 1989–2014," *Crime, Media, Culture* 11, no. 3 (2015): 281–97.

[3] These included 313 news stories, 42 editorials or signed columns, and 51 letters to the editor. In the day and age of Twitter, this doesn't sound like much. Yet, it is important to keep in mind that this was well before broadband connections were widely used. Linda S. Lichter, S. Robert Lichter, and Daniel Amundson, *The New York News Media and the Central Park Rape* (New York: The American Jewish Committee, 1989), 19.

[4] Ibid.

[5] Michael Welch, Eric A. Price, and Nana A. Yankey, "Moral Panic over Youth Violence: Wilding and the Manufacture of Menace in the Media," *Youth and Society* 34, no. 1 (September 2002): 5.

[6] Ibid., 9.

"WILDING," SUPERPREDATOR,
AND SEXUAL PREDATOR

The term *wilding* is not a legal, sociological, or forensic term. Immediately following the incident in Central Park, journalists and academics began to argue over the origins of the word. Many suggested that the term did not exist prior to April 19, 1989. In an op-ed in the *New York Times,* J. Anthony Lukas hypothesized that "wilding" was the result of a mishearing:

> Wilding. For more than a month, the word has chilled and titillated us. In two staccato syllables, it encapsulates the slithery dread many New Yorkers feel at the menace lurking out there in the dark. . . . The term came to us first through the chief of detectives, quoting one of the accused as saying, "We were going 'wilding.'" But police in the precincts had never heard the word before; nor had street kids surveyed by reporters. Some suspect that the accused actually told the police they were after "the wild thing"— a euphemism for sex—from the rap song of that name.[7]

Others involved in the case made similar arguments, and Lukas's theory has been given relatively little academic attention since then.[8] The research of literary scholar Stephen Mexal suggests otherwise. As he explains, the term "wilding'" has its etymology in the language of wilderness in early twentieth century Black

---

[7] J. Anthony Lukas, "Wilding—As American as Tom Sawyer," *New York Times,* May 28, 1989.

[8] Exceptions to this include: Susan Baker and Tipper Gore, "Some Reasons for 'Wilding,'" *Newsweek* 113, May 29, 1989; Michael Welch, Eric Price, and Nana Yankey, "Youth Violence and Race in the Media: The Emergence of 'Wilding' as an Invention of the Press," *Race, Gender & Class* 11, no. 2 (2004): 39.

literary naturalism and in hip-hop culture prior to 1989.[9] The
term was first used "critically, ironically, and strategically." In the
context of the Central Parker Jogger rape, wilding was appropriated by white people to not only connote sexual predatory
behavior, but also savagery in the sense of a lack of civilized
behavior. As Mexal explains, Central Park was conceived as a
"genteel, natural space."[10] In addition to being outraged by the
crime itself, white New York residents were also upset about how
the crime's location disrupted their understanding of an "idyllic
place."[11] Black and Latino youth "savages" had now invaded a
"civilized" white space. Thus, the term created a "multivalent
spectacle in part because of an interpretive failure on the part of
the broader public" to interpret the term ironically.[12]

The use of the term *wilding* heightened the spectacle of the
case and incited moral panic by linking the actions of the individuals suspected of the crime to those of untamed beasts or
wild animals. Doing so allowed members of the general public
to suspend empathy for the people accused, through tactics of
disidentification. The implication was that Salaam, Wise, Richardson, Santana, and McCray were not fully human. A few years
after the attack, John J. DiLulio Jr. developed an untested theory
of the "superpredator" to describe the spike in juvenile crime.[13]
As explained by Carroll Boggert and Lynne Hancock of the

---

[9] Stephen J. Mexal, "The Roots of 'Wilding': Black Literary Naturalism,
the Language of Wilderness, and Hip Hop in the Central Park Jogger Rape,"
African American Review 46, no.1 (Spring 2013): 101–12. Mexal states, "Wilding
seemed to speak of a random, atavistic crime outside the transactional logic of
burglary or robbery, possessing a structure ungraspable by its bourgeois victims"
(106).

[10] Ibid., 111.

[11] Ibid., 112.

[12] Ibid.

[13] John DiLulio, "The Coming of the Super-Predators," *Washington Examiner*, November 27, 1995.

Marshall Project, DiLulio was "extrapolating from a study of Philadelphia boys that calculated 6 percent of them accounted for more than half the serious crimes committed by the whole cohort."[14] He argued that their behavior was the result of moral depravity. The idea was that like predatory animals, these young men went out hunting for victims to kill, without conscience or remorse. While DiLulio's theory was discredited in the academic community, it caught on in the media and had a lasting impact on sentencing and policy.[15] The tendency to describe and treat human beings as animals began long ago in chattel slavery. Animalistic comparisons in the media perpetuate myths of Black male bestiality in relation to white female vulnerability. Furthermore, multiple commentaries related to lynching as a form of punishment for Black bodies reemerged with this case, harkening back to chattel slavery and Jim Crow.[16]

BLACK BODIES AND WHITE GAZES[17]

African American and Latino/a people have long been depicted as threats to the social and moral fabric of the nation on screen. *The Birth of a Nation* (1915), based on Thomas Dixon's best-selling book and play *The Clansmen*, depicts freed Black men

---

[14] Carroll Bogert and Lynnell Hancock, "Superpredators: The Media Myth That Demonized a Generation of Black Youth," *The Marshall Project*, November 20, 2020.

[15] Ibid. See also Lawrence Bartley and Donald Washington Jr. "The Making of Superpredators," *The Marshall Project,* March 11, 2021.

[16] See Jim Dwyer, "The True Story of How a City in Fear Brutalized the Central Park Five," *New York Times*, May 30, 2019. Also see Sarah Burns, *The Central Park Five: The Untold Story Behind One of New York City's Most Infamous Crimes* (New York: Vintage Books, 2012), 73–74.

[17] This is a reference to the work of George Yancy. Specifically, his *Black Bodies, White Gazes: The Continuing Significance of Race in America*, 2nd ed. (Lanham, MD: Rowman & Littlefield, 2016).

as sex-crazed brutes who had to be controlled.[18] As George Yancy illustrates, "The white gaze, in *Birth of a Nation*, depicted the 'truth' of the sexually rapacious black body, which was constructed as something to be feared and controlled by white nation builders and keepers of white purity."[19] The film "render[ed] lynching an efficient and honorable act of justice and served to help reunite the North and South as a white Christian nation, at the expense of African Americans."[20] By the early twentieth century, the majority of Southern whites had seen the film. Following reconstruction, lynching was the predominant way of policing Black bodies.

A key aspect of lynching was the spectacle that it generated. As James Cone describes, people came in by the thousands to witness a lynching. They were advertised widely in the community and "were a family affair, a ritual celebration of white supremacy, where women and children were often given the first opportunity to torture Black-victims—burning Black flesh and cutting off genitals, fingers, toes, and ears as souvenirs."[21] Photographs of the white lynchers with the Black victim sold as postcards. These were mailed to relatives and friends and family members afterward. As Cone indicates, this could not have happened without the sanction of the state. The purpose of the advertisement and gathering was not only to incite terror and fear in Black people, but also to celebrate white power and dominance. It was a way of demonstrating how easily white people could kill and conquer Black people.

As interdisciplinary scholar Elías Ortega-Aponte has illustrated, the phenomenon continues today on social media with

---

[18] James Cone, *The Cross and the Lynching Tree* (Maryknoll, NY: Orbis Books, 2012), 5.

[19] George Yancy, *Look, A White! Philosophical Essays on Whiteness* (Philadelphia: Temple University Publications, 2012), 109.

[20] Ibid.

[21] Cone, *The Cross and the Lynching Tree*, 9.

the circulation of viral videos that depict violence against Black people: "The images, videos, and bits of data are circulated in digital environments in an orchestration that pits Black suffering against the white liberal gaze—that is, the historical and enduring witness of Black lives afflicted by the violence of white supremacy and the white liberal gaze that cannot empathize with this witness but seeks to explain it away."[22] As Ortega-Aponte explains, families of victims lose control over the circulation of the materials (e.g., the video of George Floyd) and the telling of the story. In this way, they have to experience the trauma over and over again as the episode of violence is replayed on the internet and its meaning debated. The materials are often "circulated through a plurality of networks without our knowledge or consent. In this way the terror . . . extends to the digital world."[23] A spectacle of neo-lynching, as Ortega-Aponte describes, is generated, destined to exist perpetually online.

During chattel slavery, lynching was less common because Blacks "were considered valuable property."[24] After the Civil War, lynching became a way of inculcating fear and establishing white dominance. After reconstruction, slave patrols evolved into modern police departments.[25] Thus, the conflation between social and moral control and crime control began early on. In the words of James Cone, "Lynchings were grounded in the religious belief that America is a white nation called by God to witness

---

[22] Elías Ortega-Aponte, "The Haunting of the Lynching Spectacles: An Ethics of Response," in *Anti-Blackness and Christian Ethics*, ed. Vincent W. Lloyd and Andrew Prevot (Maryknoll, NY: Orbis Books: 2017), 124.

[23] Ibid., 125.

[24] Cone, *The Cross and the Lynching Tree*, 4.

[25] Jamiles Lartey and Annaliese Griffin, "Race and Policing," *The Marshall Project*, October 21, 2020; Jill Lepore, "The Invention of Policing," *New Yorker*, July 13, 2020; Khalil Gibran Muhammad, "American Police," podcast audio, *NPR Throughline*, June 4, 2020. Also see Equal Justice Initiative, *Lynching in America: Confronting the Legacy of Racial Terror*, 3rd ed. (2017).

the superiority of 'white over Black.'"[26] Therefore, it became the moral duty of white Christian men to protect both the sanctity of their homes and of the white race. It is important to point out that people were lynched for small social transgressions like looking a white person in the eyes, failing to use the honorific of "mister," or knocking on a white person's front door. Yet, the greatest fear of white people—the worst crime—was race mixing or sexual intercourse between races.[27] *The Birth of a Nation* translated this religio-racial project onto the screen.[28]

In this way, media like *The Birth of a Nation* played a pivotal role in affirming and reinforcing the white moral imagination. What was written in the text and projected onto the screen did not so much create a belief system as hold up a mirror to deep-seated racialized beliefs already in place about criminality and justice. Moreover, the film and accompanying texts were extremely successful because they provided the moral justification for the policing of Black people in the form of lynching. While the National Association for the Advancement of Colored People (NAACP) protested the film's representation of Black people and organized a major campaign to have it banned, *The Birth of a Nation* played a major role in reigniting the Ku Klux Klan (KKK). Prior to the film, the KKK was a regional group in the South that had been forced to go underground by the government. When the film was released, the group capitalized upon the film's popularity and used it as a tool for recruitment. This was

---

[26] Cone, *The Cross and the Lynching Tree*, 7.

[27] Ibid., 8.

[28] "Religio-racial project" is a reference to Jeanine Hill Fletcher's use of the term in *The Sin of White Supremacy: Christianity, Racism, and Religious Diversity in America* (Maryknoll, NY: Orbis Books, 2017), chap. 1. In *The Birth of a Nation*, Flora and Margaret Cameron symbolize Southern virtue. When Gus, a freed slave, who is depicted in animalistic form, attempts to rape Flora, she commits suicide by jumping off Lover's Leap. D. W. Griffith and Thomas Dixon, *The Birth of a Nation* (Los Angeles: Triangle Film Corp., 1915).

only possible because of the new climate, in which Jim Crow, anti-immigrant sentiment, and a half-hearted condemnation of racism in the North allowed the KKK to flourish.[29] A great deal of crime media functions in a similar manner by misrepresenting the criminal justice system, normalizing injustice, and creating a spectacle on screen.

Today, true crime and fictional representations of crime regularly misrepresent the way the criminal justice system works, normalize injustice, and ignore the lived experience of persons who are incarcerated. On screen, the system is simplified. As we noted in Chapter 1, an individual is arrested, questioned by police, provided with legal counsel, and sent to a jury trial. Yet, the vast majority of criminal cases never make it to trial.[30] The accused all too often agree to plea bargains for fear of manda- tory minimum sentencing and, in some cases, confess to crimes they never committed.[31] Meanwhile, the crime and the carceral system are represented as race-neutral realities, despite what crime statistics reveal.[32] A 2020 report by the Abolitionist Law Center Court Watch indicates that less than 13 percent of the Allegheny County population (including Pittsburgh) is Black, yet 67 percent of the Allegheny County jail population is Black.[33] Moreover, news coverage and crime shows (fictional and true

[29] Alexis Clark, "How 'Birth of the Nation' Revived the KKK," History Channel, last modified July 29, 2019.

[30] Stacy L. Mallicoat, *Crime and Criminal Justice: Concepts and Controversies,* 2nd ed. (Los Angeles: SAGE Publications, 2019), 11–14.

[31] Carlos Berdejó, "Criminalizing Race: Racial Disparities in Plea-bargain- ing," *Boston College Law Review* 59 (2018): 1187; Michelle Alexander, *The New Jim Crow: Mass Incarceration in the Age of Colorblindness*, rev. ed. (New York: The New Press, 2011), 230–31.

[32] For example, the imprisonment rate for Black men is 5.7 times higher than for white males, according to a Bureau of Justice report. See E. Ann Carson, "Prisoners in 2019," Bureau of Justice Statistics, October 2020.

[33] Abolitionist Law Center Court Watch, "Cash Bail, Arbitrary Detention, and Apartheid in Allegheny County" (Summer 2020), 3.

crime) tend to focus on homicides, despite the fact that they represent a fraction of all felonies.[34] In what follows, we take a closer look at the various tactics used to normalize injustice in scripted crime media and true crime on television.

RENDERING RACISM
INVISIBLE ON SCREEN

Color of Change Hollywood conducted a major study that breaks down the representation of Black and Latinx characters in scripted crime media on major networks and streaming services.[35] The study, which looked at twenty-six scripted television shows (353 episodes), found that the majority of scripted crime dramas on major networks or platforms (FOX, NBC, ABC, Netflix, and Amazon) routinely normalize injustice through the actions of criminal justice professionals (CJPs).[36] For example, in an episode of *NCIS* called the "Party Crashers," when white CJPs sought to enter without a warrant, they called their new African American female boss, who responded: "Let me worry about the legal ramifications." In this case, illegal and immoral behavior of fictional white cops, behavior that is often directed toward Black people in real life, was affirmed by a fictional Black character.[37] No mention of race was ever made. While we do not

---

[34] Media scholars have argued that accounts of crime, across genres, tend to feature violent crime, individual perpetrators, and innocent victims. See Andrew J. Baranauskas and Kevin M. Drakulich, "Media Construction of Crime Revisited: Media Types, Consumer Contexts, and Frames of Crime and Justice," *Criminology* 56, no. 4 (2018): 681.

[35] Color of Change Hollywood, "Normalizing Injustice: The Dangerous Misrepresentations that Define Television's Scripted Crime Genre," USC Annenberg Norman Lear Center (January 2020).

[36] Ibid., 60.

[37] Ibid.

have the space to analyze adequately all roles in crime drama, it is important to note that a similar framing tactic occurs in crime media when African Americans are disproportionately cast as judges.[38] More frequently it is the case that wrong actions by CJPs are simply not acknowledged on screen. The study found that shows shied away from explicit depictions of many things prevalent in real life, such as racial profiling and racially based practices. Therefore, the impression is given that whatever a CJP does is "inherently 'right' and 'good' by virtue of it being done by a CJP."[39]

The Color of Change Hollywood team also found that scripted crime series misrepresent how the criminal justice system works, through what was not shown. In particular, long-term harms of the legal system and day-to-day practices (such as plea bargains, racial profiling, parole practices, and money bail) were not shown. Moreover, the crimes themselves were misrepresented. For example, Black women and transwomen are rarely portrayed as victims of crimes on television. In fact, the study found that representation of crime and justice on television was largely presented as race neutral.[40] Yet, this does not correlate with the experiences of Black and Latino/as or with research that has been conducted. While more uniform data collection is needed across the country, researchers at Stanford University examined nearly one-hundred-million traffic stops and found that racial bias exists when deciding whom to stop, and that police had a

---

[38] See Merlene George, "Black Skins, Black Robes . . . White Justice? Black Judges and Reality-Based Courtroom Dramas," *The Review of Education, Pedagogy, and Cultural Studies* 25, no. 1 (2003): 35–53.

[39] Color of Change Hollywood, "Normalizing Injustice," 60.

[40] Ibid., 62. This is also the case in true crime; see Ashley Duchemin, "White Women Need to Do Better: The Death of 'My Favorite Murder,'" *Bitch Media*, August 8, 2017.

higher propensity to search Black and Hispanic drivers.[41] In New York City, stop-and-frisk policing tactics disproportionately target Black and Latino/a people.[42] Yet, scripted crime drama suggests otherwise—the Color of Change Hollywood team found that 58 percent of the persons of interest on such shows were white, only 15 percent Black, and 26 percent Latino/a, Asian, and other unidentified races.[43] It is important to note that in many cases the screenwriters and producers did not clearly identify the ethnic background of nonwhite characters on screen, making it difficult to assess the distribution. Failure to distinguish among members within ethnicity groups is a white way of seeing (e.g., conflating Japanese Americans with Indian Americans). This is not surprising given that most of the screenwriters and creators examined in the study were white.[44]

Recall that the "CSI effect" stems from false representations of forensic science on the popular scripted crime drama *CSI: Crime Scene Investigation* and its numerous spinoffs.[45] The CSI franchise portrays primarily homicide investigations, beginning with the

---

[41] Researchers used the veil-of-darkness test to assess if the demographic composition of drivers who were stopped changed in the dark, when race could not be identified. Fewer Black drivers were stopped in the dark, indicating that bias is indeed present in the decision to stop. Emma Pierson, Camelia Simoiu, Jan Overgoor, Sam Corbett-Davies, Daniel Jenson, Amy Shoemaker, Vignesh Ramachandran, et al., "A Large-scale Analysis of Racial Disparities in Police Stops across the United States," *Nature Human Behaviour* 4, no. 7 (2020): 736–45.

[42] Sharad Goel, Justin M. Rao, and Ravi Shroff, "Precinct or Prejudice? Understanding Racial Disparities in New York City's Stop-and-Frisk Policy," *Annals of Applied Statistics* 10, no. 1 (2016): 365–94.

[43] Color of Change Hollywood, "Normalizing Injustice," 112. Nonidentifiable in the sense that their races were not mentioned.

[44] Ibid., 65.

[45] Steven M. Smith, Veronica Stinson, and Marc W. Patry, "Fact or Fiction: The Myth and Reality of the CSI Effect," *Court Review* 47, no. 1–2 (2011): 4–7. Also see Michael Johnson, "The CSI Effect: TV Crime Dramas' Impact on Justice," *Cardozo Public Law, Policy, and Ethics Journal* 15, no. 2 (Spring 2017): 385–412.

on-scene investigation and concluding with an individual's arrest. The shows often give a false sense of closure to each episode by solving each case within the hour, no matter the complexity. Additionally, each character can inhabit an unrealistic range of roles, such as one person being both a crime scene investigator and a lab analyst capable of performing a variety of forensic analyses. In real life, forensic analysts are trained in a specific discipline, not in all forensic techniques, and only some analysts also serve as crime scene investigators.

A great deal of true crime media plays into the sensationalism of scripted crime dramas, normalizing injustice and rendering racism invisible. Netflix's true crime documentary *Murder to Mercy: The Cyntoia Brown Story* (2020), which covers the journey of Cyntoia Brown-Long, who is biracial, from being sex-trafficked to incarceration, was created without her consent. At the age of sixteen, Brown-Long, acting in self-defense, shot and killed John Allen. Even though she was a minor, Brown-Long was tried in adult court and sentenced to life in prison. While she was in prison, film producer Dan Birman made a deal with Netflix to create a documentary about the story.[46] *Murder to Mercy* focuses largely on Brown-Long's personal journey to "redemption" and glosses over racial dynamics related to her life experience. For example, in her trial and sentencing, Brown-Long was "described as a teenage prostitute, not a trafficking victim."[47] As she recounts in her memoir, the word *trafficking* was not mentioned in conjunction with her case until years after the fact.[48] In 2019, she was granted clemency. *Murder to Mercy* includes family interviews

---

[46] Mahita Gajanan, "The History behind the Netflix Documentary 'Murder to Mercy: The Cyntoia Brown Story,'" *Time Magazine*, April 29, 2020.

[47] Cyntoia Brown-Long with Bethany Mauger, *Free Cyntoia: My Search for Redemption in the American Prison System* (New York: Atria Books, 2019), Kindle edition, 113.

[48] Ibid.

that describe Brown-Long's traumatic childhood and focuses on her personal efforts toward self-growth and transformation in prison (for example, she earned a degree while incarcerated). Yet the absence of explicit conversation on race in the film reinforces the notion that justice is doled out to those who earn it through hard work. This tricks the viewer into believing that race played little part in Brown-Long's sentencing. In this way, true crime works as a potent form of propaganda, as it renders racism invisible within the criminal justice system and reinforces the myth of meritocracy (the notion that what you have is the result of your own hard work).

While some have argued that true crime opens up space for critiquing the carceral system, the people who are incarcerated continue to "remain a very small subplot."[49] Many of the wrongful conviction stories highlighted in true crime media examine cases where the convictions have been overturned. Some stories document the cases of persons still incarcerated who were wrongfully convicted or are facing excessive punishment. Public attention garnered by the coverage may assist these individuals; after Curtis Flowers's story was told on the *In the Dark* podcast, the United States Supreme Court threw out his sixth trial conviction.[50] Yet even following the Supreme Court decision to dismiss all charges against him, District Attorney Doug Evans maintains that Flowers, who is Black, is guilty and that race does not play a role in the case. It is worth noting that

---

[49] P. E. Moskowitz, "True Crime Is Cathartic for Women. It's Also Cop Propaganda," *Mother Jones* (May/June 2020). Also see Marcos A. Hernandez, "True Injustice: Cultures of Violence and Stories of Resistance in the New True Crime," *IdeaFest: Interdisciplinary Journal of Creative Works and Research from Humboldt State University* 3, no. 1 (2019): 13.

[50] American Public Media, "The Case Against Curtis Flowers," podcast audio, *In the Dark*, June 5, 2018; Jason Slotkin, "After 6 Trials, Prosecutors Drop Charges Against Curtis Flowers," NPR, September 5, 2020.

out of the seventy-two jurors involved in the six trials, sixty-one were white.[51]

In addition, these narratives tend to highlight information that emphasizes the innocence of the individual instead of engaging the complex relationship between innocence and culpability. Such representation not only reinforces an expectation of innocence for exoneration, it also fails to account for the profound ways in which the carceral system fails those who are most vulnerable in our society. This is a problem for multiple reasons. First of all, this framework ignores the lived experience of people who are incarcerated. Regardless of culpability, once a person is in the system, they can get written up for small infractions, such as accidentally bumping into an officer in an overcrowded hallway. Too many write-ups can affect a person's sentencing or parole. Second, in true crime narratives, exoneration is often predicated upon wrongful convictions of innocent parties, rather than on overly harsh sentencing. No one is completely innocent in a society that tries juveniles as adults and incarcerates them for life without the possibility of parole.[52] Young people have just begun living their lives, but such sentencing suggests that moral growth is not possible. People like Brown-Long are cast as guilty before they even enter the courtroom.

In this way, true crime narratives encourage viewers to accept morally wrong actions (e.g., harsh sentencing, cash bail, and pressure to accept plea deals) by CJPs in the name of justice. It also explains, in part, why so many white people were stunned to learn about the deaths of Breonna Taylor or George Floyd. The true crime framework presents such cases as isolated incidents

---

[51] Sharyn Alfonsi, "How Curtis Flowers, Tried Six Times for the Same Crime, Was Saved from Death Row," CBS News, January 3, 2021.

[52] For more on this, see Equal Justice Initiative, "Cruel and Unusual: Sentencing 13- and 14-year-old Children to Die in Prison" (2008).

instead of a systemic problem. In this framework, white people are then outraged by miscarriages of justice (as they should be), and demand better from the system without investigating the root causes of those injustices and how their complicity in those causes contributes to wrongful convictions and harsh sentencing.[53] We struggle not only to see the whole, but our place within it. As James Baldwin stated decades ago: "White people were, and are, astounded by the holocaust in Germany. They did not know they could act that way. But I very much doubt whether Black people were astounded."[54] White people have become so accustomed to a vision of themselves as good and upstanding people that they are stunned to see images of themselves killing with impunity. True crime reinforces this kind of privileged self-understanding, both by normalizing the moral wrongs of CJPs and by its silence on systemic racism. More to the point, viewers are not empowered to do anything about evil because they don't have to. The problem is solved for them; it is either resolved on screen or pushed out of mind.

REENTRY: STORIES UNTOLD

Another thing we don't see in true crime media is the disproportionate number of Black and Latino/as convicted of drug charges while whites are released with warnings for the same offenses or never even arrested. Netflix's 2021 documentary *Crack, Cocaine, Corruption, and Conspiracy* by Stanley Nelson is an exception to this tendency. The disparities began in the 1980s, when the war

[53] The Innocence Project cites leading causes of wrongful convictions aa eyewitness misidentification, prosecutorial misconduct, flawed forensic science, and false confessions. Many of these played out in the case of the Central Park Jogger. The CJPs questioned the teens without their parents present and elicited false confessions. Lyndsie will further unpack the relationship of racial bias and forensic science in Chapter 6.

[54] James Baldwin, *The Fire Next Time* (London: Michael Joseph, 1963, 1968), 62.

on drugs targeted and punished Black communities already rav-
aged by the crack epidemic. The inequality is evident now when
we retrospectively examine the crack epidemic and compare it to
how the current opioid epidemic is being handled from a health
perspective, rather than a punishment model. It is no coincidence
that crack largely affected Black communities, while opioids are
impacting white communities. As author Michelle Alexander
describes in *The New Jim Crow*, the war on drugs in the 1980s
criminalizes the actions of people of color although all races
use and sell drugs at similar rates.[55] For example, although Black
Americans are no more likely than white Americans to use illegal
drugs, they are "6 to 10 times more likely to be incarcerated for
drug offenses."[56] Drug offenses accounted for two-thirds of the
rise in federal incarcerations and more than half the increase in
state incarcerations between 1985 and 2000.[57]

As Alexander describes it, the war on drugs functions as a
racial caste system. Black men and women enter the system as a
result of police techniques that disproportionately target people
of color. Following arrest, many of these individuals receive inadequate counsel, undergo pressure to plead guilty, and ultimately
receive harsher sentences due to laws related to drug offenses,
like mandatory minimums. After serving the sentence, individuals face additional legal sanctions that have a lasting impact.[58] As
Alexander explains:

> [The legal system] operate[s] collectively to ensure that
> the vast majority of people convicted of crimes will never
> integrate into mainstream, white society. They will be

---

[55] Alexander, *The New Jim Crow*, 14–16.

[56] J. Netherland, H. B. Hansen, "The War on Drugs That Wasn't: Wasted
Whiteness, 'Dirty Doctors,' and Race in Media Coverage of Prescription
Opioid Misuse," *Culture, Medicine, and Psychiatry* 40, no. 4 (2016): 669.

[57] Alexander, *The New Jim Crow*, 14–22.

[58] Ibid., 229–30.

discriminated against, legally, for the rest of their lives—denied employment, housing, education, and public benefits. Unable to surmount these obstacles, most will eventually return to prison and then be released again, caught in a closed circuit of perpetual marginality.[59]

In the words of one returning citizen: "It seems like I was given a scarlet F to wear around on my forehead the rest of my life. You know, it's an F for felon and nobody will touch it with a 10-foot pole and so it seems like kind of a lifetime conviction."[60] With well over 90 percent of individuals eventually released from prison, how easy is it to return to society?[61] What do returning citizens need? Some of the challenges to reentry include acquiring housing and employment, and are often further complicated by a lack of family support (or needing to support one themselves), health and addiction problems, and difficulty tending to basic life needs and obtaining ongoing legal services.

CJPs often view recidivism rates as the primary indicator of successful reentry. (*Recidivism* refers to an individual's return to prison as a result of committing another crime or violating a condition of their release.) Numerous academic studies have been conducted on the topic of reentry. One study defined success as "being discharged from parole by 3 years after release."[62] In another study, male returning citizens viewed successful reentry as obtaining stable employment, owning property or a

---

[59] Ibid., 230.

[60] Heather Hlavka, Darren Wheelock, and Richard Jones, "Exoffender Accounts of Successful Reentry from Prison," *Journal of Offender Rehabilitation* 54, no. 6 (2015): 411.

[61] Joan Petersilia, *When Prisoners Come Home: Parole and Prisoner Reentry* (New York: Oxford University Press, 2003), 3.

[62] Stephen J. Bahr, Lish Harris, James K. Fisher, and Anita Harker Armstrong, "Successful Reentry: What Differentiates Successful and Unsuccessful Parolees?" *International Journal of Offender Therapy and Comparative Criminology* 54, no. 5 (2010): 667–92.

business, giving back to the community by helping others and being able to provide for themselves and their families.[63]

While there are many barriers to success, and recidivism rates are high, the people that should be designing programs for reentry and dictating policy are the returning citizens themselves.[64] This is important because many of those who have been incarcerated have also been victimized by the system. In other words, true crime media projects a perpetrator/victim binary, when the reality is much more complex. For example, approximately one-third of people (nearly 250,000) in US jails are awaiting trial. These are people who have not been convicted of anything. The primary reason for their detention is inability to post bond or bail. Extensive research shows that Black and Latino/a people are more likely to face higher bail amounts.[65] They are also less likely to be released without cash bail. Moreover, as we have mentioned, white people who consume opiates are less likely to be charged with a crime, and more likely to be treated as patients. These are just a few scenarios. While people who have committed crimes are held accountable, the system is not equitable. For many people the "punishment" does not fit the crime, and they are not given a chance for reintegration into society. All of this raises larger questions about the purpose of prisons. Consider,

---

[63] Tia S. Andersen, Deena A. Isom Scott, Hunter M. Boehme, Sarah King, and Toniqua Mikell, "What Matters to Formerly Incarcerated Men? Looking beyond Recidivism as a Measure of Successful Reintegration," *The Prison Journal* 100, no. 4 (2020): 488–509.

[64] Mariel Alper, Matthew R. Durose, and Joshua Markman, *2018 Update on Prisoner Recidivism: A 9-year Follow-up Period (2005–2014)* (Washington, DC: US Department of Justice, Office of Justice Programs, Bureau of Justice Statistics, 2018). A longitudinal study conducted by the Bureau of Justice Statistics tracked recidivism rates for 401,288 state prisoners released in 2005 and found that during the nine-year follow-up, five out of six were re-arrested at least once.

[65] Zhen Zeng, *Jail Inmates in 2018* (Washington, DC: US Department of Justice, Bureau of Justice Statistics, 2018). Traci Schlesinger, "Racial and Ethnic Disparity in Pretrial Criminal Processing," *Justice Quarterly* (February 2007).

for example, the stories of two members of the Elsinore-Bennu Think Tank (EBTT), excerpted from the podcast *Criminal (In) Justice.* The podcast purposefully chose not to use the names of "Mr. R." and "Mr. F" to protect their privacy.[66]

Mr. F was sentenced to life in prison without parole as a juvenile, due to Pennsylvania's mandatory sentencing laws.[67] Upon his release after spending forty-nine years in the carceral system, he was lucky to have family support that assisted him with securing shelter, food, clothing, and appropriate identification so that he could obtain a job. Parole officers would tell men being released to obtain an ID or to attend a job fair, without providing any further assistance. Although not showing up to a job fair would be a parole violation, directions to where it was or how to get there were not provided.

As Mr. R was sentenced at fourteen years old and spent thirty-eight years in prison, he had a similar experience to Mr. F. He shares that parole officers would say, "Go get your ID, but they couldn't say here's how you get it, here's what you need to get it, here's how you get there because honestly we didn't even know how to get from one place to the other." When confronted with these challenges, Mr. F's family told him to ask the officers for help. His response, "I'll find a way, because if this is going to

---

[66] David Harris, "#131 Re-entry: The Real Experience," podcast audio, *Criminal (In)justice,* February 9, 2021. We asked Mr. F, Mr. R, and David Harris over Zoom if we could include part of the podcast in this book. We are grateful for their permission and everyone's assistance.

[67] These are laws that largely were enacted during the "superpredator" era. John R. Mills, Anna M. Dorn, and Amelia Courtney Hritz, "Juvenile Life without Parole in Law and Practice: Chronicling the Rapid Change Underway," *American University Law Review* 65 (2015): 535. We are aware that the examples in this chapter include juveniles; this presents a myriad of unique challenges and further complicates ideas related to criminality. Given the focus of this book, adequate discussion of the treatment of juveniles in the criminal justice system cannot be included. Additional information can be found at Equal Justice Initiative, "All Children Are Children: Challenging Abusive Punishment of Juveniles" (2017).

be a pattern in regards to just telling me what to do, not helping me do it, I'm going to have to get used to it." Mr. F. and
Mr. R. did more than get used to it; they succeeded, making a
regular contribution to society and the local community. In their
current work, Mr. F. and Mr. R. collaborate with other returning citizens and community members to reimagine and reshape
reentry in Pittsburgh.

During the podcast interview, they both shared that there
were a number of people who had never been through the experience telling them what they needed and what they should
be doing. Nonprofit agencies set up to help with the reentry
process tried to fit everyone into a box without accounting for
individual needs. For example, Mr. R, already employed by this
time, had to take time off work to attend a job fair. At the fair,
he was offered a lower-paying job and told if he did not take the
position, he would be in violation. Luckily, he was able to work
with the parole officer and supervisor to keep his higher-paying
job and not be in violation just because he was supposed to follow the prescribed steps outlined by individuals without reentry
experience. Rather than providing real support, some agencies
touted their success in order to obtain additional grant funding
but never actually helped the returning citizens obtain a job or
housing. As Mr. R shares, "Whatever you do for me without me,
you do to me. Reentry should be by, of, and for re-entrants." He
further explains, "What the people need to realize is that when
you hear that title ex-convict, re-entry, returning citizen, that
does not immediately make for a bad guy, a rapist, a murderer, a
thief, or someone who committed crimes or someone worthy of
prison, that's really not the case."[68] All too often, returning citizens are defined by their history instead of their future potential.

Standing up in the face of adversity, figuring out a way to
succeed, and building a network to help move forward rather

---

[68] Harris, "Re-entry: The Real Experience."

than reverting to old ways truly represents resilience. The stories of Mr. R and Mr. F are two examples out of countless stories of returning citizens overcoming adversity to successfully reenter society, stories that never make it into true crime media.[69] The returning citizens we have met in the EBTT are smart, intelligent, and compassionate individuals. We have learned from their example how to listen, teach, and imagine justice afresh. What is really devastating is how much beauty and wisdom are taken from communities and our schools when people with so much creative and innovative talent are locked up.

HUMAN DIGNITY
AND THE EXONERATED FIVE

The case of the Central Park Jogger ended with the wrongful convictions of Yusef Salaam (15), Korey Wise (16), Kevin Richardson (14), Raymond Santana (14), and Antron McCray (15). Thirteen years after the crime and wrongful imprisonment of the five teens, DNA testing proved Matias Reyes was the individual who committed the rape. And while police and prosecutors had been busy focusing on the wrong people, Reyes raped other women. Although the Central Park Five case was "resolved," it had a lasting impact on the daily lives of those wrongfully convicted and their families. *When They See Us*, Ava DuVernay's dramatized retelling for Netflix of the Central Park

---

[69] Jia Wertz, director, *Conviction* (New York City Film Academy, 2021). The stories of successful reentry typically only appear on-screen if the individual was wrongfully convicted. For example, the documentary "Conviction" focuses on the reentry of exoneree Jeffrey Deskovic, who was wrongfully convicted of rape and murder at seventeen years old. After sixteen years in prison, he was released with nothing—no reentry services exist for individuals released after being wrongfully convicted. Although reentry services do exist for other returning citizens, the effectiveness of such programs is questionable, with bureaucratic requirements and checklists often substituting for the guidance and support that are truly needed.

Jogger case, is meant to showcase the perspectives of the men and their families from the arrest, through trial, in prison, and upon release. In an interview, McCray, Salaam, Richardson, Wise, and Santana describe how the film was the first time they truly understood what the others went through. Many white people hold the misconception that all Black people know one another and experience racism in the same way. But although these five had similar experiences, there were differences that they never talked about.[70] One of the tactics of the prosecution was to keep the young men separated. White people have employed similar tactics for centuries in United States, including but not limited to the separation of families within chattel slavery, denial of education, and so on.[71]

DuVernay states that the title of the movie was an effort to embrace the humanity of the men and to reframe the narrative from the "Central Park Jogger Case" to the "Central Park Five" and finally to the "Exonerated Five."[72] As DuVernay tweeted prior to the film's release:

> Not thugs. Not wilding. Not criminals. Not even the Central Park Five. They are Korey, Antron, Raymond, Yusef, Kevin. There are millions of young people of color who are blamed, judged and accused on sight. May 31. A film in four parts about who they really are. WHEN THEY SEE US.[73]

---

[70] Mark Ritchie, director, *Oprah Winfrey Presents: When They See Us Now*, Southpaw Production (2019). For those unfamiliar with the case, the only two who knew each other prior to the arrest and conviction were Yusef Salaam and Korey Wise. The rest had never met.

[71] For more, see M. Shawn Copeland, *Knowing Christ Crucified: The African American Religious Experience* (Maryknoll, NY: Orbis Books, 2018), chap. 1.

[72] Michelle Darrisaw, "Ava DuVernay's 'When They See Us' Looks at the Central Park Five—Here's What to Know," *Oprah Daily*, September 20, 2019.

[73] Ava DuVernay (@Ava), Twitter, March 1, 2019.

It was important in the film to humanize Korey, Antron, Raymond, Yusef, and Kevin. To see what really happened to them.
When individuals are locked up, hidden away in prison cells, they
remain invisible to us. And everyone loses.

The Central Park Jogger case accentuates the inadequacies of
the criminal justice system in the United States and its lifelong
impact on survivors of racial trauma. While most white people
acknowledge the limitations of the criminal justice system in
this particular case, they do not acknowledge the ways in which
white fear of Black sexuality operates in the background. This
case highlights the devastating cost of injustice at multiple levels. And while true crime media can raise awareness of these
injustices, a number of issues remain as these shows continue to
assume a victim/perpetrator binary and fail to convey that the
Exonerated Five, Mr. R., Mr. F., and Cyntoia Brown-Long are
survivors of a system that betrays us all. On television shows,
problems are tied up neatly, allowing white onlookers a way out
of their own complicity in anti-Blackness and shutting the door
to more complex stories of survival, resistance, and healing.

A study of the *New York Times* articles about the Central Park
Jogger case shows the shift from guilt to wrongful conviction
language as the years progressed. At the time of the crime, news
outlets used a shocking violence narrative so readers would
have the sense of "it could have been me." Other violent crimes
occurred that week but didn't garner the same level of media
attention because they lacked the interracial dimension.[74] The
later miscarriages of justice narratives examine how the criminal
justice system victimized those individuals that were wrongfully convicted. Why can't these stories be told by engaging the

---

[74] Greg Stratton, "Transforming the Central Park Jogger into the Central
Park Five: Shifting Narratives of Innocence and Changing Media Discourse
in the Attack on the Central Park Jogger, 1989–2014," *Crime, Media, Culture*
11, no. 3 (2015): 281–97.

complexities of the case, in which multiple victims-survivors exist in different ways? For example, in the Central Park Five case, Trisha Meili is a victim-survivor of the assault and rape by Matias Reyes. Korey Wise, Raymond Santana, Yusef Salaam, Keith Richardson, and Antron McCray are also survivors of the carceral state.

In a 2021 *New York Times* opinion piece, members of the Exonerated Five wrote that "what people may not realize is that what happened to us isn't just the past—it's the present."[75] This quotation reminds us all that the racial stereotypes presented in *The Birth of a Nation* still exist today. Stories of lived experiences testify to the violence of the carceral state. Wisdom from individuals reentering society is needed, as their lived experiences can have a profound influence on others in similar situations or in prevention strategies. Many formerly incarcerated individuals advocate for improved practices across the criminal justice system that will prevent future injustices. They often work to help other returning citizens by aiding in reentry efforts. For example, exoneree Jeffrey Deskovic went on to complete his law degree, create a foundation, and, so far, has helped free seven wrongfully convicted individuals as well as contributing to legislative abolition of the death penalty in Connecticut.[76]

During the third part of *When They See Us*, Kevin Richardson reflects, "I never thought I would grow up to be hated."[77] No child grows up expecting to be viciously hated by people who don't even know them. Similar sentiments are shared by returning citizens facing stereotypes and stigmatization due to past

---

[75] Yusef Salaam, Kevin Richardson, and Raymond Santana, "We Are the 'Exonerated 5.' What Happened to Us Isn't Past, It's Present," *New York Times*, January 4, 2021.

[76] Wertz, *Conviction*.

[77] Ava DuVernay, director, *When They See Us, Part 3*, Tribeca Productions (2019).

incarceration, without being acknowledged for their humanity. True crime media traditionally fails to highlight the story of individuals who committed a crime and return to society after serving their sentence or being released on parole. We don't get to see the stories of individuals who resist the temptations to reengage in criminal activity, who face adversity daily as they navigate a variety of challenges trying to reintegrate into society, and who nevertheless work to mentor others and promote a better society. These are the stories we should lift up.

Certainly, the media can have a positive influence on public understanding of the justice system. Notable media outlets such as *The Marshall Project* and *Crime Report* provide journalism that documents the realities of the criminal justice system and strives to increase public understanding, but media's invention and propagation of terms like *wilding* and *superpredator* aim to enhance the "info-tainment" value of crime stories. While the true crime genre has created a space for critique of the criminal justice system, in a way that scripted dramas like *COPS* and *NCIS* do not, larger questions remain as to whether the genre sustains deeper engagement in the systemic causes of racial injustice. In 2020, a number of films and series were released that highlight injustices in the criminal justice system,[78] but the question remains: Does the release of these films and shows represent a shift in media viewing that will lead to system changes, or is it merely an attempt to enhance viewership based on the current cultural environment? As Bryan Stevenson and the Equal Justice Initiative assert on the Equal Justice Initiative home page, "We must truthfully confront our history of racial injustice before we can repair its painful legacy." As such, we must confront systemic racial injustice if we hope to achieve a criminal justice system that is equitable for all citizens.

---

[78] Examples can be found on Netflix within the *Black Lives Matter* Collection.

6

BLIND (IN)JUSTICE: BIAS AND FORENSIC SCIENCE

This past semester, Elisabeth and I had the opportunity to co-teach a class on the topic of this book with Jamar Williams, a member of the Elsinore-Bennu Think Tank (EBTT). We began with Bryan Stevenson's *Just Mercy: A Story of Justice and Redemption*, in which he documents the foundation of the Equal Justice Initiative and his involvement in a number of cases that confront racial injustice in the criminal justice system.[1] The main case Stevenson discusses involves Walter McMillian, a Black man in Alabama, who was wrongfully convicted for the murder of Ronda Morrison, a white woman. His conviction relied heavily on false testimony from the prosecution witnesses and from illegal suppression of exculpatory evidence. He spent six years on death row before his conviction was overturned in 1993.[2] In one assignment for the class, we asked the students to reflect upon a person in the text to whose story they could relate. We had a number of responses, some better than others. Yet, in a

---

[1] The Equal Justice Initiative, "Just Mercy," www.eji.org.
[2] Bryan Stevenson, *Just Mercy: A Story of Justice and Redemption* (New York: Spiegel & Grau, 2015).

room full of future criminal justice professionals, nurses, and psychologists, none of them chose to write about the people in the book who worked in their future profession. Perhaps this is because Stevenson flips the narrative so that those who most fully embody humanity are the people behind bars and the ones who put them there cannot hide their complicity with injustice.

As I contemplated the reflection question we posed to students, I realized that I related most to the police officers and prosecution lawyers who contributed to the wrongful conviction of Walter McMillian. Acknowledging this reality opened my eyes to the education and training I received during the early part of my forensic science career. The curriculum included a very limited discussion of bias and error, but today, extensive research has documented various types of bias that infiltrate all levels of the criminal justice system.[3] This chapter highlights the impact of bias specifically within forensic science. Although touted as a tool to prevent miscarriages of justice through an unbiased analysis, forensic science (through misapplication, misconduct, or mistake) has been cited as a contributing factor in 24–52 percent of wrongful conviction cases.[4] While the true impact of forensic science as a contributing factor in wrongful convictions is highly debated between lawyers and scientists, we (forensic scientists) cannot absolve ourselves entirely of wrongdoing.[5] Forensic science plays a dual role in the system, and only focusing on the good (contribution to rightful conviction) without fixing the

---

[3] See Gregg Barak, Paul Leighton, and Jeanne Flavin, *Class, Race, Gender, and Crime: The Social Realities of Justice in America* (Lanham, MD: Rowman & Littlefield, 2010); Radley Balko, "There's Overwhelming Evidence That the Criminal Justice System Is Racist. Here's the Proof," *Washington Post*, June 10, 2020.

[4] Innocence Project, "Overturning Wrongful Convictions Involving Misapplied Forensics."

[5] Simon A. Cole, "Forensic Science and Wrongful Convictions: From Exposer to Contributor to Corrector," *New England Law Review* 46 (2011): 711.

bad (contribution to wrongful conviction) is like turning a blind eye to injustice.[6]

COGNITIVE BIAS AND FALLACIES

As social psychologist Jennifer Eberhardt explains, "Bias, even when we are not conscious of it, has consequences that we need to understand and mitigate. The stereotypical associations we carry in our heads can affect what we perceive, how we think, and the actions we take."[7] The broad category of cognitive biases relates to unconscious beliefs or perceptions. Generally, "The science of implicit cognition suggests that actors do not always have conscious, intentional control over the processes of social perception, impression formation, and judgment that motivate their actions."[8] The architecture of the brain works in various ways to increase processing, and therefore as an individual we are not always cognizant of the underpinnings of our decisions.

As legal researchers noted in 2015, "For the most part, for decades the courts have accepted forensic evidence as scientific, objective, and impartial, as well as highly reliable and validated."[9] This notion of objective impartiality went largely unexamined until the late 2000s. The 2009 National Research Council report *Strengthening Forensic Science in the United States: A Path Forward*

---

[6] For more information, see Brandon Garrett, *Convicting the Innocent* (Cambridge, MA: Harvard University Press, 2011); John M. Collins and Jay Jarvis, "The Wrongful Conviction of Forensic Science," *Forensic Science Policy and Management* 1, no. 1 (2009): 17–31; Gerald LaPorte, "Wrongful Convictions and DNA Exonerations: Understanding the Role of Forensic Science," *National Institute of Justice Journal*, no. 279 (2018): 1–16.

[7] Jennifer Eberhardt, *Biased: Uncovering the Hidden Prejudice That Shapes What We See, Think, and Do* (New York: Viking, 2019), 49.

[8] Anthony G. Greenwald and Linda Hamilton Krieger, "Implicit Bias: Scientific Foundations," *California Law Review* 94, no. 4 (2006): 946.

[9] Sherry Nakhaeizadeh, Itiel E. Dror, and Ruth M. Morgan, "The Emergence of Cognitive Bias in Forensic Science and Criminal Investigations," *British Journal of American Legal Studies* 4, no. 2 (2015): 527.

recommended more research dedicated to identifying bias and human errors in forensic science examinations as well as the implementation of bias mitigation processes.[10] Research studies and improved practices have followed, but not without resistance.

A 2017 study that surveyed over four hundred forensic scientists across twenty-one different countries indicated that examiners believe bias is an issue in forensic science (71 percent), but only 25 percent recognize the impact bias has on their own judgments.[11] This study further found that examiners believe bias mitigation can be achieved by ignoring expectations. For instance, if examiners have a prior expectation that the evidence will match a reference prior to analysis, examiners believe that making a conscious effort to disregard this expectation is enough to guard against the possible influence of bias on the analysis. This willpower mentality fails to account for the natural brain processes involved in decision-making that are unrelated to a person's conscious intentions.[12]

Research has defined fallacies related to bias that arise due to a lack of understanding about the nature of cognitive bias: illusion of control, blind spot, expert immunity and impartiality, ethical issue, "bad apples," and the notion that technology eliminates bias.[13] The *illusion of control fallacy* relates to the willpower mentality, but having a conscious intention is not enough to combat bias—specific action is required as well. The 2017 study discussed above demonstrates the *blind spot bias,* or the inability

---

[10] National Research Council, *Strengthening Forensic Science in the United States: A Path Forward* (Washington, DC: National Academies Press, 2009), 111–25.

[11] Jeff Kukucka, Saul M. Kassin, Patricia A. Zapf, and Itiel E. Dror, "Cognitive Bias and Blindness: A Global Survey of Forensic Science Examiners," *Journal of Applied Research in Memory and Cognition* 6, no. 4 (2017): 452–59.

[12] Ibid.

[13] Itiel E. Dror, "Cognitive and Human Factors in Expert Decision Making: Six Fallacies and the Eight Sources of Bias," *Analytical Chemistry* 92, no. 12 (2020): 7999.

for individuals to recognize their own biases. The *ethical fallacy* is related to the incorrect belief that bias only affects corrupt individuals or is a result of deliberate misconduct. While intentional misconduct cases exist, they differ from cognitive bias effects, which are "not about such ethical issues of personal character, integrity, or intentional misconduct."[14] Similarly, the *"bad apple" fallacy* blames the expert for the error, calling into question the expert's competency. Yet even the most trained examiners are susceptible to bias, due to how the human brain works. No one is immune from bias, not even experts, which relates to the *expert immunity fallacy*. In some ways expert decision-making may in fact be more susceptible to certain types of bias. While experience and training often enhance quick and accurate decision-making, the same cognitive processes can lead to prior (false) assumptions before a decision is made.[15]

Another fallacy relates to the belief that the *use of technology* can eliminate bias. This fallacy is perpetuated through media representations. For example, when you watch *CSI* on television, a forensic analyst inputs a fingerprint into the database, yielding one match. Yet, in real life, a list of potential matches is returned that must be carefully reviewed by the examiner. People often think that technology can eliminate all error, which is of course not true. While technology can reduce bias, human biases are not entirely removed because the systems themselves are "built, programmed, operated, or interpreted by humans."[16]

BIAS IN FORENSIC SCIENCE

Itiel Dror, a researcher in the field of cognitive neuroscience, has become one of the leaders dedicated to researching and

---

[14] Ibid.
[15] Ibid., 7998–99.
[16] Ibid.

improving forensic science practices in order to reduce the impact of bias. He developed a taxonomy of bias sources, which he represented as a pyramid. The base or foundation of the pyramid relates to human nature; the middle relates to environment, culture, and experience; and the top represents potential sources of bias related to case-specific information.[17] The sources of bias at the top are specific to forensic science; the analysis of evidence in a given case may introduce bias depending on the type of data that is being evaluated. For example, a saliva swab does not include potential biasing information, but a handwritten note could—the information included in the note could provide contextual clues as to the crime or the individuals involved.

Another case-related source of bias relates to reference materials. In most forensic disciplines, evidence from the crime will be compared to reference material about persons of interest or other information. At this stage of the analysis, it is imperative that the examination and comparison be based on the actual evidence, rather than being driven by the references.[18] For instance, trying to find the fingerprint features of the person of interest in the case results in a biased examination because it means they are looking for specific features, rather than identifying all the features that might be present. Another level of bias at the case level is task-irrelevant case information. Often the police provide irrelevant contextual information about the case when they submit evidence for forensic analysis, and such information that is not required for the forensic analysis might bias the examination. For example, the police might include the fact that a person of interest confessed, has a criminal record, or was identified by an eyewitness.[19] Again, it is important that the evidence alone be

---

[17] Ibid., 7999–8003.

[18] Itiel E. Dror, "Human Expert Performance in Forensic Decision Making: Seven Different Sources of Bias," *Australian Journal of Forensic Sciences* 49, no. 5 (2017): 1–7.

[19] Ibid.

analyzed with scientific techniques in order to draw conclusions devoid of external information or contextual information not required for analysis.[20] The sources of bias related to case information are currently the most studied within forensic science. As these sources are related to case-specific information, the potential impact of bias at this level is the most controllable. Potential mitigation techniques will be explored later.

Numerous studies have examined the impact of contextual information across forensic science disciplines. A systematic literature review conducted in 2019 revealed twenty-nine research studies related to cognitive bias and forensic science.[21] One study examined what happened when fingerprint examiners were given a pair of fingerprints that they had previously reported as a definitive match. In addition to the evidence, examiners were falsely informed that the fingerprints were those from the Madrid bombing case that erroneously identified Brandon Mayfield. Only one out of the five participants reported the fingerprints as a match; the remaining examiners declared a non-match or stated that there was insufficient information to make a conclusion, even though all five had previously reported them to be a definitive match. The analysts were unaware that they were being tested, and the study, although it utilized a small sample size, revealed the effect of contextual information on the objective analysis.[22] Other examples of extraneous information include past

---

[20] The President's Council of Advisors on Science and Technology's "Report to the President, Forensic Science in Criminal Courts: Ensuring Scientific Validity of Feature-Comparison Methods" (2016) further emphasizes the importance of scientific validity in forensic science and the potential impact of cognitive bias.

[21] Glinda S. Cooper and Vanessa Meterko, "Cognitive Bias Research in Forensic Science: A Systematic Review," *Forensic Science International* 297 (2019): 35–46.

[22] Itiel E. Dror, David Charlton, and Ailsa E. Péron, "Contextual Information Renders Experts Vulnerable to Making Erroneous Identifications," *Forensic Science International* 156, no. 1 (2006): 74–78.

convictions, police theories, confessions, or eyewitness testimony. All of this information is irrelevant to the forensic examination and may bias analyses.[23]

ENVIRONMENTAL AND HUMAN FACTORS

Moving down the taxonomy, the sources transition from case specific to the environment and individuals involved. Itiel Dror further defines numerous sources of bias that relate to the environment, culture, and experiences of the analyst. Potential sources of bias include base rate expectations, organizational factors, education and training, and personal factors. Base rate expectations refer to the impact an examiner's past experiences have on expectations for current and future cases. Forensic scientists become experts based on their education and experience. From past experience working similar cases, analysts develop certain beliefs and assumptions that transfer to the current case they are processing, even though such expectations have nothing to do with the current case. Base rate expectations will be further explored later.

Examiners also experience numerous biases based on their work environment.[24] One study demonstrated that forensic examiners experience adversarial allegiance, or a propensity to side with the prosecution or defense based on which side retained them as an expert. In analyzing the same evidence, they reached different conclusions depending on whether they believed they were an expert for the prosecution or defense.[25] Another work

---

[23] Brett O. Gardner et al., "Do Evidence Submission Forms Expose Latent Print Examiners to Task-Irrelevant Information?" *Forensic Science International* 297 (2019): 236–42.

[24] Dror, "Cognitive and Human Factors," 8002.

[25] Daniel C. Murrie, Marcus T. Boccaccini, Lucy A. Guarnera, and Katrina A. Rufino, "Are Forensic Experts Biased by the Side That Retained Them?" *Psychological Science* 24, no. 10 (2013): 1889–97.

environment factor that can influence and introduce bias relates to organizational factors. "Almost all publicly funded laboratories, whether federal, state, or local, are associated with law enforcement. At the very least, this creates an inherent conflict-of-interest and leads to legitimate concerns of objectivity and bias."[26] For example, many labs under a management structure related to law enforcement or a prosecutor's office may think of themselves as members of the investigative or prosecution team, thereby influencing "objective" scientific analysis.[27] Additional organizational factors that may introduce bias include "time pressure, expectations to reach certain results, stress, [and] budget controls." Other sources of bias include the training the examiner receives and the motivation of the examiner, along with personal factors such as individual beliefs, response to stress, and personality.[28]

At the foundation of the hierarchy (base of the pyramid), Dror identifies human nature factors. This refers to the bias that relates to the cognitive architecture of the brain. As represented by the pyramid, this source of bias is placed at the base given the fundamental nature of human cognition that affects all individuals.[29] I believe this type of bias is the most significant, yet it is also the hardest to mitigate. People naturally use mental shortcuts (heuristics) to solve problems or make judgments more efficiently.[30] The

---

[26] Suzanne Bell, Sunita Sah, Thomas D. Albright, S. James Gates, M. Bonner Denton, and Arturo Casadevall, "A Call for More Science in Forensic Science," *Proceedings of the National Academy of Sciences* 115, no. 18 (2018): 4541–44.

[27] Paul C. Giannelli, "Independent Crime Laboratories: The Problem of Motivational and Cognitive Bias," *Utah Law Review* 2010, no. 2 (2010): 247. For more information related to the management structure of forensic science laboratories, see Sandra Guerra Thompson, *Cops in Lab Coats: Curbing Wrongful Convictions through Independent Forensic Laboratories* (Durham, NC: Carolina Academic Press, 2015).

[28] Dror, "Cognitive and Human Factors," 8002.

[29] Ibid.

[30] Amos Tversky and Daniel Kahneman, "Judgment under Uncertainty: Heuristics and Biases," *Science* 185, no. 4157 (1974): 1124–31.

use of "heuristic thinking, while generally beneficial, can also produce systematic errors in judgment, especially where strong prior expectations exist."[31] A nonprofit called Project Implicit, founded in 1998 by researchers from multiple universities, has created a variety of implicit association tests to educate individuals and reveal hidden biases based on "thoughts and feelings outside of conscious awareness and control."[32]

RACIAL BIAS IN FORENSIC SCIENCE

The information and examples presented thus far provide evidence that a variety of different biases can potentially affect forensic science domains. But no specific examples related to the impact of racial bias have been presented. The almost nonexistent examination of the impact of racial bias on forensic science disciplines must be rectified.

A study published in 2021 did examine the role of racial bias in forensic pathology through historical and experimental data.[33] Death certificates for children under six were collected from one state spanning a ten-year period. The researchers examined cases where the manner of death was unnatural, either an accident or homicide. Deaths designated as natural or undetermined were excluded from further analysis. Results indicated a higher rate of homicide designations for Black children compared to accidental death designations for white children. The researchers constrain these results, stating, "We must be careful in drawing conclusions

---

[31] Saul M. Kassin, Itiel E. Dror, and Jeff Kukucka, "The Forensic Confirmation Bias: Problems, Perspectives, and Proposed Solutions," *Journal of Applied Research in Memory and Cognition* 2, no. 1 (2013): 45.

[32] See "Take a Test," Project Implicit website.

[33] Itiel Dror, Judy Melinek, Jonathan L. Arden, Jeff Kukucka, Sarah Hawkins, Joye Carter, and Daniel S. Atherton, "Cognitive Bias in Forensic Pathology Decisions," *Journal of Forensic Sciences* (February 20, 2021).

about bias from these archival data, especially given that the ground truth of how these children actually died is unknown. For example, it is possible that Black children die from homicide more often than White children."[34]

In order to further explore potential contextual information bias, over 100 forensic pathologists were provided with a hypothetical case along with medically irrelevant contextual information.[35] The case involved the death of a young child who was either Black and cared for by the mother's boyfriend, or white and cared for by the grandmother. The race of the caretaker was not disclosed. When pathologists were given the same medical information, but varied race conditions, their conclusions related to the manner of death varied. When presented with a Black child, pathologists were five times more likely to list the death as a homicide rather than as an accident. Conversely, when presented with a white child, pathologists listed the death as an accident more than as a homicide. Although this study cannot determine whether the race of the child and/or the caretaker relationship affected the death determination, the results indicate that irrelevant contextual information affected the decision. This study is the first of its kind to examine the existence of racial bias in forensic pathology. The possible source of bias could be related to the unconscious racial bias of the pathologist or a bias based on base rate expectations, where pathologists through past experience have an expectation that in these types of cases a homicide manner of death is most likely for Black children.[36]

Studies and documentation highlighting racial bias throughout the criminal justice system are widespread. Arrest rates document

---

[34] Ibid.

[35] Ibid.

[36] Ibid.

the disparity between the number of minorities arrested compared to Caucasians or the disparity in bond/bail amounts and jail/prison sentences for people of color.[37] Why, then, has forensic science barely examined racial bias within its function? As I've described earlier in the book, forensic science is situated within the criminal justice system and is charged to be above all the processes and biases that may exist within the system. Forensic scientists are meant to analyze evidence using scientific methods in an unbiased manner, and then report the results. But the evidence submitted comes from law enforcement, and the reports are often used in court proceedings to support the prosecution's case. If racial bias exists at the law enforcement level and at the court proceeding level, does that mean racial bias exists within forensic science as well? Have we avoided this type of examination because the information related to the race of the suspects involved in these cases ostensibly has no bearing on the scientific testing of the evidence? Perhaps, but bias studies have shown that cognitive bias exists in forensic science and that contextual case information shared by police can influence results. Why are we afraid or unwilling to do the research? If as a discipline forensic science claims racial bias does not have an effect, we need to perform studies to see if that's really the case.

Additionally, I hypothesize that the impact or influence of racial bias will vary between forensic disciplines, requiring an examination within each discipline. The results from the forensic pathology study above indicate that racial context can have an influence, but different results may be obtained for other forensic disciplines where race is not inherently connected to the evidence. For example, when analyzing fingerprints, trace evidence, or bullet casings, the analyst does not need to know the race of the individuals connected to the evidence in order to perform

---

[37] Balko, "Criminal Justice System Is Racist."

the analysis, compared to forensic pathologists who visually see the race of the victim. While significant progress has been made in the attempt to reduce bias in forensic science, there must be an ongoing effort to further examine and mitigate confirmation and contextual bias. Additionally, studies are needed to examine the influence of task-irrelevant case information on inherent bias related to race.

A June 2020 message from the president of the American Academy of Forensic Sciences (AAFS) to all members reads:

> Today I address you, the Academy membership, greatly saddened and overwhelmed with questions as to how social injustice and the disturbing deaths of George Floyd, Ahmaud Arbery, Breonna Taylor, and others are continuing to occur. Our Nation is embroiled in civil unrest and demand for action against racism, intolerance, and injustice that continue to exist in our country. Because we serve many communities and help the forensic sciences support truth in evidence, we cannot allow inaction and silence in our daily work or in our own professional community of the Academy. We must address persistent biases in all of our communities.[38]

AAFS is one of the leading forensic science organizations, with a global network of members representing the various disciplines within forensic science. This message shares an important sentiment. I agree that "action against racism, intolerance, and injustice" must be taken.[39] I also believe that action can start from within by conducting racial bias studies in each discipline in order to evaluate and understand the potential impact of racial bias across forensic science.

---

[38] Jeri D. Ropero-Miller, "President's Spotlight-June 2020," *Academy News,* blog, American Academy of Forensic Sciences, June 8, 2020.
[39] Ibid.

MITIGATING BIAS

Many potential sources of bias exist in forensic science, both those that are directly related to the discipline as well as those that affect everyone. The recognition of these sources is a critical first step to mitigate the potential impact of bias on forensic analysis. One of my colleagues, a steadfast lawyer focused on conviction integrity, often shares the sentiment with colleagues and students that lawyers focus on achieving justice, while forensic scientists focus on finding truth. Forensic science's integration in the criminal justice system should assist in upholding conviction integrity by bringing science into the courtroom to help prevent wrongful convictions and contribute to proper convictions. This requires the use of validated scientific methods in conjunction with bias education and mitigation.

Forensic scientists must implement processes and procedures that are as unbiased as possible, using sound scientific methods to analyze evidence and report results. But even with the best of intentions, unconscious bias can affect interpretation, particularly in ambiguous cases without clearcut answers. In order to combat bias, its existence must be recognized and action must be taken. Willpower is not enough to combat the potential effects of bias. Procedures should be implemented to ensure the examination proceeds from the evidence to the reference (i.e. person of interest) and never the reverse. This means that a forensic examiner should never look at a reference profile prior to analyzing the evidence profile because it can bias the analysis of the evidence profile. For example, if a DNA examiner looks at the peaks present in a person of interest's DNA profile before examining the evidence, the examiner may be looking to identify the reference in a mixed-evidence profile. One common technique to reduce bias and ensure examiners analyze evidence prior to reference samples is by implementing a process called linear sequential unmasking. Essentially in this technique analysts examine and characterize case evidence before making any comparisons to reference material.[40] Additional steps to combat bias include implementing blinding, masking, double-blind, and verification procedures when possible.[41] Another technique includes comparing evidence to a series of possible references rather than a singular reference, similar to police lineups. Further procedures can reduce exposure to irrelevant contextual information by limiting communication between officers, analysts, and lawyers by means of a case manager who controls the flow of information. This process eliminates the potential for police officers to share task-irrelevant case details, thereby reducing potential contextual bias by the examiner.[42] Dror's taxonomy indicates that the largest potential source of bias is related to human nature; therefore, forensic scientists must continually be cognizant and proactively work to identify potential bias and mitigate potential effects. Increased education, training, and research related to bias are important steps, along with developing additional techniques to reduce the impact of bias.

As I think back to the reflection assignment we posed to students and my own connection with the criminal justice professionals who contributed to the failures of justice, I am reminded of Bryan Stevenson's words: "Walter's case taught me that fear and anger are a threat to justice; they can infect a community, a state, or a nation and make us blind, irrational and dangerous."[43] I think about this threat to justice through our blindness and

---

[40] Itiel E. Dror, William C. Thompson, Christian A. Meissner, Irv Kornfield, Dan Krane, Michael Saks, and Michael Risinger, "Context Management Toolbox: A Linear Sequential Unmasking (LSU) Approach for Minimizing Cognitive Bias in Forensic Decision Making," letter to the editor, *Journal of Forensic Sciences* 60, no. 4 (2015): 1111–12.

[41] Dror, "Cognitive and Human Factors," 7998–8004.

[42] Ibid.

[43] Stevenson, *Just Mercy*, 313.

biases on three levels: as a forensic scientist, as an educator, and as a citizen. Specifically, in forensic science, failure to acknowledge our racial biases as members of the criminal justice system can have grave consequences on the outcome of cases, and thus on people's lives. Techniques and procedures can be implemented to limit certain types of bias, such as confirmation bias, by removing irrelevant contextual information from the analysis. Forensic confirmation bias refers to "the class of effects through which an individual's pre-existing beliefs, expectations, motives, and situation context influence the collection, perception, and interpretation of evidence during the course of a criminal case."[44]

As an educator, I must constantly recognize the biases I'm bringing into the classroom or transferring to the students. As Elisabeth and I discussed the reflection paper assignment, we realized that our initial reaction was anger and frustration—we thought that we were doing an amazing job in the classroom and this was a failure on the students' part. And as I step back and reexamine that assignment and their responses now, I recognize that we brought our own biases to assessing the work, looking for the students to confirm our expectations. And in fact, the students' responses clarified the need to teach racial bias in the classroom.

Finally, as a citizen, whether serving as a member of a jury or talking to a family member about current events, I am bringing my own biases to that situation. As a member of society, I must be vigilant of other types of inherent bias based on human nature. These ingrained thoughts, attitudes, and perceptions, which I may not even be aware of, require deeper reflection and examination.

SEEKING JUSTICE

When I think of the American criminal justice system, the figure of a blindfolded female wielding her sword and scales often

---

[44] Kassin et al., "The Forensic Confirmation Bias," 45.

comes to mind as a symbolic representation of blind justice. But I also think of cartoon representations where Lady Justice is peeking from behind her blindfold, reminding us that she is not truly blind.[45] A historical examination reveals that justice was previously represented with an open line of sight associated with the "eye of justice." It was not until the sixteenth century and the Protestant Reformation that the blindfold appeared, changing the narrative from one in which sight was essential for viewing the facts to one in which the blindfold represented impartiality.[46] Debates regarding the representation of justice with and without the blindfold endure, but I bring it up in order to evoke the paradox that exists between the need to recognize bias (see it) and the fact that the methods to mitigate it often involve blinding techniques, particularly in the sciences. Failing to recognize the impact of bias within the criminal justice system leads to blind injustice.

In less than twenty years, the understanding of the potential impact of bias in forensic science has greatly expanded, leading to an increase in documented research and techniques for bias mitigation. The eight sources of bias defined by Dror provide a clear explanation of biases specific to forensic science as well as bias sources common to everyone based on human nature. Even with this progress, however, the work must continue. No longer can experts hide behind the blind spot fallacy, failing to recognize their own biases, nor can the general public claim expert immunity. Research reveals the existence and potential impact of bias within various forensic science domains because the research is set up in a manner where the true answer of the analysis is

---

[45] Dennis E. Curtis and Judith Resnik, "Images of Justice," *The Yale Law Journal* 96, no. 8 (1987): 1727–72.

[46] Marcílio Franca, "The Blindness of Justice: An Iconographic Dialogue between Art and Law," in *See*, ed. Andrea Pavoni, Danilo Mandic, Caterina Nirta, and Andreas Philippopoulos-Mihalopoulos (London: University of Westminster Press 2018): 159–96.

known. For example, the effect of contextual information can be specifically examined to determine if task-irrelevant information affects the ultimate conclusions. When analyzing evidence from real cases, it is much harder to isolate the impact of bias because there is no ground truth.

Forensic science's role in the criminal justice system requires evidence analysis based on sound scientific methods and bias mitigation techniques. Bias is extremely complicated; there are many kinds of bias. The impact of bias varies among forensic disciplines and individuals based on education, training, and personal factors. We must also ask, while enhanced discussions of bias and error now exist, are there other factors that contribute to injustice?

As a human being and person of faith, I know that racial bias has deadly consequences. The question is to what degree the discipline of forensic science is affected by racial bias. I believe that one of the biggest (and most pressing) questions forensic scientists will have to come to terms with in the future is that of the ethics for the standard of objective neutrality in the face of white supremacy. How do I teach future forensic scientists to participate in the criminal justice system using unbiased techniques, while struggling to address the systemic inequalities embedded within the current administration of the American criminal justice system? I struggle with these questions as a scientist, an educator, and an individual. While I don't have all the answers, I do know that it takes work and a continued commitment to strive for a justice system that provides justice for all. These and other big questions animate my work and drive me to stay in conversation with theologians like Elisabeth and communities like the EBTT. As a forensic scientist, educator, and an individual, I am not immune to bias; neither can I be blind to my personal impact on the administration of justice, whether that impact is direct or indirect.

7

WHITE GOODNESS, REDEMPTION, AND THE SEARCH FOR JUSTICE

I (Elisabeth) have often wondered if there is a substantive differ-ence between someone like Amy Cooper and myself. There is a great deal of disdain toward Amy Cooper and other "Karens" in white liberal circles.[1] While I may not have called the cops on a (Harvard-educated) Black man bird watching in Central Park and lied about being assaulted, there are plenty of other ways in which white educated liberal women betray BIPOC communities.

On April 20, 2021, a jury found Derek Chauvin, the former Minneapolis police officer who knelt on George Floyd's neck for nine minutes, guilty on all counts: second-degree murder, third-degree murder, and second-degree manslaughter. Chauvin

---

[1] I follow Shannon Sullivan's use of the term *good white liberal,* which does not designate party affiliation. Rather it refers to the "'good' white people whose goodness is marked by their difference from the 'bad' white people who are considered responsible for any lingering racism in a progressive, liberal society." See Shannon Sullivan, *Good White People: The Problem with Middle-Class White Anti-Racism* (Albany: State University of New York Press, 2014), Kindle edition, 3.

143

murdered Floyd the very same day that Amy Cooper called the
cops on Christian Cooper. And as reported by the *New York
Times*, a mere twenty minutes prior to the announcement of
the Chauvin verdict, sixteen-year-old Ma'Khia Bryant was shot
and killed by police in Columbus, Ohio.[2] On April 22, 2021, the
US Supreme Court in *Jones v. Mississippi* rejected limits on life
sentences for juveniles. Several days later, the news cycle shifted
to new data on climate change and the upcoming Oscars.

We white liberal Christians work pretty hard to differentiate
ourselves from people like Amy Cooper. Doing so allows us to
preserve our own sense of moral goodness and innocence. This is
comforting because we can deflect attention away from ourselves.
This is likely why true crime media is comforting to so many
white people; it makes sharp distinctions between good and
evil, innocence and guilt, and victim and perpetrator—and the
"good" always prevails. Christianity has not always been a help
in this regard. Pastor and writer Nadia Bolz-Weber explains the
problem well: "There's a popular misconception that religion,
Christianity specifically, is about knowing the difference between
good and evil so that we can choose the good. But being good
has never set me free the way truth has."[3] Yet, as Bolz-Weber explains, "instead of contrasting good and evil, he [Jesus] contrasted
truth and evil. I have to think about all the times I've substituted
being good (or appearing to be good) for truth."[4] White Christians are often so focused on striving to appear to be good that
we fail to notice our collusion with evil. Like Bolz-Weber, we
are called to reflect upon the times we have substituted appear-

---

[2] Kevin Williams, Jack Healy, and Will Wright, "'A Horrendous Tragedy':
The Chaotic Moments Before a Police Shooting in Columbus," *New York
Times,* April 21, 2021.
[3] Nadia Bolz-Weber, *Pastrix: The Cranky, Beautiful Faith of a Sinner and Saint*
(New York: Jericho Books, 2013), 73.
[4] Ibid.

ing good for the truth. The truth in the Christian gospels is that salvation consists in the liberation of all people here on earth. This truth is what will set us free. I am not entirely convinced that white Christians would recognize the truth of who we are and who we are called to be, because we have spent so much time pretending. Too many white Christians are caught up in maintaining their own image of moral goodness. This can happen in all kinds of places, including in religiously affiliated or progressive-minded organizations.

Sociologist Sarita Srivastava interviewed a number of feminists who worked in antiracist organizations. Based upon these interviews, she illustrates how white empathy can go wrong, "reinforc[ing] the notion of the universally kind, helping white woman."[5] For example, a participant shared a story in which her organization was trying to deal with turmoil over accusations of racism: a white board member "showed up at the women of color caucus meeting to voice her support, but instead spoke about herself and cried."[6] As Srivastava notes, inherent in her public display of revulsion toward racism was also a display of inherent goodness. While this kind of public emotional display is meant to be helpful, it is actually a display of power. In the background lies an "imperial history of respectability and benevolence on the part of white women."[7] White desires to be seen as innocent and good must be understood within a historical context marked by imperialism benevolence and missionary conquest. (Recall the conversation about whiteness and niceness in Chapter 4.) Throughout history, white people have said they were helping, saving, or educating people of color. Instead, we

---

[5] Sarita Srivastava, "'You're Calling Me a Racist?' The Moral and Emotional Regulation of Antiracism and Feminism," *Signs* 31, no. 1 (2005): 44.

[6] Ibid., 44.

[7] Ibid., 45.

have Christianized, enslaved, displaced, and stolen land from native cultures. Christopher S. Collins and Alexander Jun remind us that emotional claims are not neutral in conversations about racial justice.[8]

While white people must learn how to recognize their pain and address it in healthy ways, sharing is not always appropriate in public spaces. Instead, Collins and Jun note, white people need to learn the "art of holding other people's pain."[9] Another example of empathy gone wrong is when white people steal emotional attention. Collins and Jun point to instances where white people inappropriately reveal experiences of divorce or molestation in the context of classroom conversations focused on diversity and racial justice.[10] Attention is diverted away from the topic at hand, thereby minimizing the systemic racism that happens to so many people of color.

Returning to Amy Cooper, theologian Bryan Massingale assesses the situation as follows:

> Amy Cooper reveals what W. E. B. Du Bois calls "the souls of white folks." Because, to quote James Baldwin again, facing the truth "would reveal more about America to Americans than Americans want to know." Or admit that they know . . . that Amy Cooper is not simply a rogue white person or a mean-spirited white woman who did an odious thing. Yes, we should and must condemn her words and actions. But we don't want to admit that there is a lot more to this story. That she knew, we all know, that she had the support of an unseen yet very real

---

[8] Christopher S. Collins and Alexander Jun, *White Out: Understanding Privilege and White Dominance in the Modern Age* (New York: Peter Lang, 2017), 20.

[9] Ibid., 29.

[10] Ibid., 29, 22.

apparatus of collective thoughts, fears, beliefs, practices, and history.[11]

From Massingale's point of view, Amy Cooper and I are not all that different. He is right.

As Massingale writes, Amy Cooper assumed "that the frame of 'Black rapist' versus 'white damsel in distress' would be clearly understood by everyone: the police, the press and the public"; "that a Black man had no right to tell her what to do"; and "that the police officers would agree."[12] Finally, "She assumed that even if the police made no arrest, that a lot of white people would take her side and believe her anyway."[13] Addressing his white readers, Massingale notes that they probably know, "even without being explicitly told, that being white makes life easier," that "white life matters more than Black life," and that "by being white you could make things hard—much harder—for others. Especially Black folks."[14] As a white woman, I know these things too. Again, the moral problem is not a lack of awareness. The moral problem is linked to a desire to maintain and conceal white goodness.

GOOD WHITE CHRISTIANS

White Christians like to think of themselves as good people. Throughout history, white abolitionists and civil rights activists like Levi Coffin, Jeannie Graetz, and Tim Wise have worked in

---

[11] Bryan Massingale, "The Assumptions of White Privilege and What We Can Do about It: Amy Cooper Knew Exactly What She Was Doing. We All Do. And That's the Problem," *National Catholic Reporter*, June 1, 2020, ncronline. org.

[12] Ibid.

[13] Ibid.

[14] Ibid.

the struggle for racial justice.[15] Yet, good white people are also racist people. As writer Ijeoma Olou states, "Black and brown people are burdened with a presumption of guilt and dangerousness that is evident in myriad ways."[16] The racism that upholds white supremacy is insidious, polluting nearly every aspect of US life. Oluo explains, "There is no way you can inherit white privilege from birth, learn racist white supremacist history in schools, consume racist and white supremacist movies and films, work in a racist and white supremacist workforce, and vote for racist and white supremacist governments and not be racist."[17] Racism is in the air we breathe, the clothes we wear, the books we read, the food we eat, and the homes we inhabit. Racism informs the decisions white people make on a daily basis. It shapes who we vote for, where we send our children to school, and what we believe is important. Racist actions, beliefs, practices, and systems hurt people, regardless of intention.

When I was an undergraduate in college, I was interested in African Studies and African American Studies. I took classes in African and African American history, literature, and dance. Richard Wright's *Native Son*, Jewelle Gomez's *Gilda Stories*, and Nawal El Saadawi's *Woman at Point Zero* haunted me in the best ways possible.[18] Yet, I approached the words *racism, whiteness,* and *white supremacy* as terms to memorize, concepts to get "right" on exams—not as lived realities essential to my own survival. Today, many good-intentioned white liberal people approach racism and white privilege in a similar fashion. In the days following

---

[15] For other examples see Boyd Drick, *White Allies in the Struggle for Racial Justice* (Maryknoll, NY: Orbis Books, 2015).

[16] Equal Justice Initiative, "Segregation in America" (2018).

[17] Ijeoma Oluo, *So You Want to Talk about Race* (New York: Basic Books, 2019), Kindle edition, 218.

[18] Richard Wright, *Native Son* (New York Harper Perennial, 1998); Jewelle Gomez, *The Gilda Stories* (Ithaca, NY: Firebrand Books, 1991); Nawal El Saadawi, *Woman at Point Zero*, trans. Sherif Hetata (Atlantic Highlands, NJ: Zed Books, 1975, 1983).

the death of George Floyd, Black-owned bookstores were scrambling to keep up with the demand for antiracist literature. White liberals attended lectures, watched films, and went to protests in an effort to understand, to help, to listen, and, ultimately, to do antiracism "right." Yet, there is a profound difference between being interested in learning about racism, becoming educated about it, and living in its harsh reality.

When we think about white racists, people like Amy Cooper, Derek Chauvin, and members of the Proud Boys often come to mind. Yet, as Sullivan and others have argued, white liberals and white supremacists are cut from the same cloth.[19] The challenge is that white liberals often fail to see that they are just as much a part of the problem as white supremacists, because "their ignorance often poses as knowledge, making it all the more insidious."[20] In particular, all too often white people try to flee their white identity by ignoring it, whitewashing history, bypassing controversial topics, or adopting strategies that work to maintain their own moral goodness. Sullivan describes this mindset as follows: "Those white people (the lower class) are racist; we middle-class whites are not like them; therefore we are not racist."[21] Similarly, I could think to myself, Amy Cooper is a racist, but I am not like her. Therefore, I am not racist. Sometimes it is much more subtle, such as when a white progressive asks a question in the form of a statement when a critical race scholar comes to campus as a means of demonstrating their knowledge. As Massingale points out, there is a profound difference between feeling uncomfortable and feeling threatened. Learning about racism might make white people feel uncomfortable, but we are not actually being threatened.[22] We are being asked to expand our self-understanding and our understanding of the world.

---

[19] Sullivan, *Good White People*, 5.

[20] Ibid.

[21] Ibid.

[22] Massingale makes this point in "White Privilege."

Learning about and being interested in racism, organizing events, or attending rallies is good and important work. I am not suggesting that white people should stop doing these activities. Yet, this does not form the basis of white allyship. In fact, as I have grown in my own understanding, I've learned that because of the insidious nature of whiteness,[23] white allyship is not something white people get to decide about. Black Latino/as, Asians, and Indigenous people decide about white allyship. This is important to realize because all too often, white people flee their whiteness. As Sullivan states, it is critical for white people to "consider themselves bound by [whiteness], and they need to acknowledge the particular constraints that their whiteness places on them to best serve as white allies of people of color."[24] To many white people, this can feel like a Catch-22, or a "White-22," to use Collins and Jun's term. A *White-22* is when white people see non-action as perpetuating an injustice, but they fear that the wrong action might make it worse.[25]

For white people, learning how to live into the uncertain space of a White-22 is part of what it means to be uncomfortable. It is always possible that the antiracist efforts of white people will make situations worse. Given the myriad ways in which white people have refused to listen to the desires and needs of people oppressed throughout history, there is a good probability that actions of well-intentioned white people may contribute to the problem of racism. However, the silence of white people in the face of racial hegemony endorses the status quo. There can be no neutrality in the face of violence. The only way out of the White-22 is to center the voices and ideas of black and brown people. Recall Mr. R's experience with community organizations, discussed in Chapter 5. While these organizations likely

---

[23] Sullivan, *Good White People*, 11.

[24] Ibid., 12.

[25] Collins and Jun, "White Out," 46.

had the honest desire to serve returning citizens, they ended up using Mr. R's intellect to further their own goals instead of helping him. This is a common problem when we consider missionary approaches to charitable work. White people and white-led organizations must engage in serious discernment as to whether they are helping or doing more harm in the community. As in the case with Mr. R, the intention was to help. Yet, good intentions were not enough; what mattered was how the actions of the organization impacted Mr. R's lived experience. The organization did not help Mr. R by compensating him for his time and talent; instead, it benefited from them itself.

As Collins and Jun remind us, "Claims of compassion fatigue, of trying but not being accepted, feeling paralyzed, and saying 'it doesn't matter what I do' are all ways in which White 22 actually becomes another strategy for maintaining White dominance."[26] This is because compassion fatigue, when articulated by dominant groups, arises out of relationships marked by dominance and subordination, in which the white person is saying "I am exhausted from helping you with your intractable problems." The notion here is that of a white savior complex, which stems from a desire to be known as a good white person.[27] Claiming paralysis means that nothing can be done; it is akin to saying that white dominance must continue. In the case of Mr. R, what would have been helpful is for those in positions of leadership to take a step back and let Mr. R lead. After all, he would know what returning citizens need. This, of course, would require major restructuring of organizations. But as Collins and Jun suggest, the first step for white people should be "to sit down. Be quick to listen more and slow to speak. Be prepared to be a

---

[26] Ibid., 48.

[27] Ibid., 29. Sullivan also makes this point in *Good White People*, 15. I understand that women are often placed in roles of service. However, I want to caution that undue attention to gender in the context of racism can work to distract attention from the issue at hand.

little uncomfortable."[28] White people do not always need to be in the lead. It is past time to center the voices of those who are closest to the problem when addressing it.

ABSOLUTION, ATONEMENT, AND RETRIBUTION

From the vantage point of Christian theologies, the seductive power of white alliances challenges white people to *stop asking Black people for absolution of white guilt and assurances of white goodness.* Christians have become very conditioned to the idea that justice before a righteous God requires acquittal or absolution of sin and is linked to sacrificial notions of punishment. For some, this can make it seem like "guilt disappears as if by magic."[29] While the Christian tradition houses a multiplicity of different images of sin, redemption, and justice, variations of Anselm's theory of atonement as satisfaction for sins persists within the public and popular imagination. Anselm likens his understanding of atonement (or "at-one-ment") to a feudal economy, in which human beings are like serfs who owe complete obedience to their master (God). Sin, in the form of disobedience, puts us in debt to God and challenges God's honor. To restore God's honor

---

[28] Collins and Jun, "White Out," 54.

[29] Katharina von Kellenbach, "Guilt and Its Purification: The Church and Sexual Abuse," *CrossCurrents* (September 2019): 238. As Amy Levad points out, while the Roman Catholic Church has three rites of reconciliation (individual, communal, and public), the focus remains on private confession. This is inadequate for addressing the social and systemic nature of evil. See Amy Levad, *Redeeming a Prison Society: A Liturgical and Sacramental Approach to Justice* (Minneapolis: Fortress Press, 2014), 105–8. Moreover, Christopher Pramuk argues, absolution of guilt in terms of the sin of whiteness is not clearcut, as it involves "guilt by common heritage." In this case, contrition cannot even begin until we take full account of the terrors of anti-Blackness and the ways in which whiteness shapes white faith formation. See Christopher Pramuk, "'Strange Fruit': Black Suffering/White Revelation," *Theological Studies* 67 (2006): 366–72.

and "re-order the beauty of the universe," God seeks satisfaction through Christ's death.[30] In the cross, salvation is effected once and for all, and virtue is marked by self-sacrifice and obedience: "There can, moreover, be nothing that a man may suffer voluntarily and without owing repayment of debt—more painful or more difficult than death. And there is no act of self-giving whereby a man may give himself to God greater than when he hands himself over to death for God's glory."[31] Yet, as Elizabeth Johnson points out, no one has ever claimed Anselm's theory as official church doctrine.[32] While much has been written regarding the interpretation of Anselm's economy of salvation and its effects and application, it is dangerous to have a "single story" about atonement, justice, and sin, especially one that can be "exploited to claim that punishment is obligatory and suffering is necessary."[33]

While scholars have pointed out that punishment and satisfaction are distinct within Anselm's thought, as Katie Grimes and Kathryn Getek Soltis illustrate, such a framework is dangerous in light of "Christianity's reliance upon the metaphor of slavery to describe the relationship between God and humanity."[34] Given the power inequities and white domination within the United States, obedience cannot really be voluntary for those who are

[30] Anselm of Canterbury, "Why God Became Man," in *Anselm of Canterbury: The Major Works*, ed. Brian Davies and G. R. Evans, 260–365 (New York: Oxford University Press, 1998), 283, 288.

[31] Ibid., 331.

[32] Elizabeth Johnson, *Creation and the Cross: The Mercy of God for a Planet in Peril* (Maryknoll, NY: Orbis Books, 2018), xiii.

[33] See Kathryn Getek Soltis, "Mass Incarceration and Theological Images of Justice," *Journal of the Society of Christian Ethics* 31, no. 2 (2011): 119. Also see Kathryn Getek Soltis and Katie Walker Grimes, "Order, Reform, and Abolition: Changes in Catholic Theological Imagination on Prisons and Punishment," *Theological Studies* 82, no. 1 (2021): 97–98.

[34] Soltis and Grimes, "Order, Reform, and Abolition," 97.

of a lower caste.[35] Further, womanist theologian Nikia Smith
Robert argues that Anselm's economy of salvation has "normal-
ized interpretations of scapegoating logic and reified racialized
pathologies of punishment that undergird penal systems of sacrifice from plantation to the penitentiary" in the United States.[36]

Drawing upon the work of Michelle Alexander, Robert
contends that prisons are an extension of slavery and that
they create a new racial caste. Therefore, "it is critical to hold
together Christian interpretations of punishment and social
contexts to understand the relationship between Jesus' sacrifice
and the scapegoating of Black bodies in an overlapping system
of sacrifice."[37] In other words, criminalized Black bodies (as a
lower social caste) are imaged as social pollutants "in need of
cleansing through discipline and punishment to restore law and
order to society."[38] In this way, the association of sin as a "social
blemish to blot out with sacrifice . . . is a theological burden for
racialized bodies."[39] While scholars contend that the Anselmian
logic of satisfaction can be separated from his understanding of
punishment, Robert rightly states that "a-historical orientation
of doctrinal claims is dangerous for Black bodies."[40] Robert's
main point is that dominant narratives of atonement and sin
within Western Christianity operate within the context of white
domination and anti-Blackness.

---

[35] Ibid.

[36] Nikia Smith Robert, "Penitence, Plantation and the Penitentiary: A
Liberation Theology for Lockdown America," *The Graduate Journal of Harvard
Divinity School* 12 (2017): 41.

[37] Ibid., 52.

[38] Ibid., 54.

[39] Ibid.

[40] Ibid., 52. Feminist theologians have made similar claims regarding inti-
mate violence. See, for example, Rita Nakashima Brock and Rebecca Parker,
Proverbs of Ashes: Violence, Redemptive Suffering, and the Search for What Saves Us
(Boston: Beacon Press, 2001).

What Anselm of Canterbury may have actually meant with his atonement theory is *not* the most pressing theological or moral question of today.[41] What we should be asking is: "How do we overturn the system so that Black bodies are no longer branded as a sacrifice for the sake of white superiority but are transformed to the fullness of their humanity for the realization of liberation?"[42] In her theology and ministry, Robert constructs a "Liberation Theology for Lockdown America" in which suffering is not redemptive, and centers the experiences of incarcerated Black mothers.[43] Her theological vision holds together in tension the cross as a site of retribution (so as to acknowledge the ways in which Black people have been and continue to be crucified by the carceral state) and a site of resistance, which highlights the agency of those who are incarcerated. Robert points out that among those in the first Christian community were criminals, because Jesus was crucified alongside them.[44] In fact, Jesus himself was considered to be a criminal in the eyes of the Roman government. By extension, Christians are called to understand Jesus as a person who is incarcerated today and executed by the state. Christians are called to "share in radical acts of resistance" to state-sanctioned violence.[45]

However, the logic that undergirds Anselm's notion of justice can become a tool for justifying white exceptionalism. In Robert's words: "Without a lower class, Anselm would have no serfs to sacrifice to restore the Lord's honor, the Antebellum south would have no Black bodies to lynch to preserve white goodness,

---

[41] Soltis makes this point in "Mass Incarceration and Theological Images of Justice" when she states, "Even so, the adjudication between restoration and retributive justice is not wholly sufficient because it continues to regard the offender as individually responsible and individually accountable" (119).

[42] Robert, "Penitence, Plantation, and the Penitentiary," 57.

[43] Ibid., 55–64.

[44] Ibid., 58.

[45] Ibid., 60.

and America would have no criminals to imprison to safeguard the privilege and power of dominant society."[46] The Anselmian insistence on cleansing of sin or Christianizing (whitewashing) becomes a way of demarcating the pure from the impure, creating a caste within Christian communities. In accepting this paradigm, Christians humiliate and vilify the subaltern so that the more powerful can be venerated.[47] Yet, as Robert argues, within Christian tradition there are multiple ways of interpreting sin and salvation. Christians do not have to accept a logic of sacrifice in order to understand God's redeeming work in the world.[48] This work is at the very heart of her ministry, Abolitionist Sancturary, which seeks to empower and equip Black churches to "create sanctuary for Black women, mothers, and system-impacted communities."[49] Doing so requires making connections between "emancipatory religious values and abolitionist principles [with] public policies and transformative justice strategies that center the communal flourishing of poor Black mothers and their families beyond prisons, policing and punishment."[50]

RETELLING THE STORY OF JUSTICE

There is a famous TED Talk called "The Danger of a Single Story," in which Nigerian novelist Chimamanda Ngozi Adichie explains the problem of racialized essentialism.[51] She describes growing up in Nigeria and reading British and American children's literature, in which the characters were white, had blond

---

[46] Ibid., 52.

[47] Ibid., 47.

[48] Ibid., 42–45.

[49] Personal communication with Rev. Dr. Nikia S. Robert on May 20, 2021. For more information about this, see "Abolistionist Sanctuary" on Robert's website, www.nikiasrobert.com.

[50] Ibid.

[51] See Chimamanda Ngozi Adichie, "The Danger of a Single Story," TED Talk, 2009.

hair, talked about the weather, and drank ginger beer. When Adichie began to write her own stories, they also included foreigners who were "white and blue-eyed, they played in the snow, they ate apples, and they talked a lot about the weather."[52] She goes on to explain that single stories have been created of Africa as a place of "negatives, difference, of darkness" that is marked by war, HIV/AIDS, and poverty. For Adichie, single stories are reductive in nature as they essentialize unfamiliar people and places. Single stories are dangerous because "they are incomplete. . . . They make one story become the only story."[53] The real issue, as my colleague Melissa Browning writes, "is not whether the story is true or untrue, but that it lacks the complexity and context needed to adequately dialogue with the issue at hand."[54]

Stories matter, including the stories we tell with our lives and our faith. Stories can invite compassion and create community, and they can be vehicles for social change. Yet, stories are dangerous when they "pretend to be more than [they are]."[55] Immediately following the jury's verdict in the Derek Chauvin case, the media proclaimed to the American public that justice had been served. Headlines read: "The law delivered justice to George Floyd. Policy makers are next."[56] Yet, this is not justice. Womanist theologian Kim Harris responds to the verdict:

> I feel that accountability was served. But, justice? It's going to take a long way toward justice. Justice is about right relationships, and we have a long way to go to right relationships. . . . We have to get to the root of what is happening

---

[52] Ibid. Also see Melissa D. Browning, "Teaching on the Streets: Engaged Pedagogy after an Execution," *Perspectives in Religious Studies* 46, no. 4 (2019): 449.

[53] Adichie, "The Danger of a Single Story."

[54] Browning, "Teaching on the Streets," 450.

[55] Ibid., 452.

[56] Stephen Collinson, "The Law Delivered Justice to George Floyd. America's Political Leaders Are Up Next," *CNN*, last updated April 21, 2021.

in our culture and understand that only a change in culture is going to really help us move to being anti-racist. We need to examine our individual consciences, but we also have to examine, collectively, our church conscience.[57]

We have a lot of growing to do as individuals, as a church, and as a nation. As Kate Ott reminds us, "ethics requires growth." Moral decision-making is more than following a set of rules; it is about "responding creatively to otherness."[58] While rules and norms have their place in society, morality is not simply about following them or choosing between good and bad. It is more about building authentic relationships and finding better solutions than about choosing the perfect response. It is about learning how to filter out the "white noise" so that you can show up with integrity, to the best of your ability, each day. You have to discern who and what deserves your attention. People make moral decisions and moral commitments on a daily basis through their actions (and inactions). The big question is whether these commitments are ones that you can stand by and stake your integrity on.

By and large, true crime tells a single story about crime and justice, one that reinforces white alliances and white goodness. In this story, law and order are restored when "perpetrators" are punished. In this framework, justice is a "zero-sum game in which the deliverance of victims hinges upon the punishment of offenders."[59] We saw this in Chapter 2 in the context of Ted Bundy's case and also in the Steubenville, Ohio, rape case, in

---

[57] In Ricardo da Silva, "Forum: 7 Black and Latino Catholics Respond to the Conviction of Derek Chauvin," *America: The Jesuit Review of Faith and Culture*, April 22, 2021.

[58] Kate Ott, *Christian Ethics for a Digital Society* (Lanham MD: Rowman & Littlefield, 2018), 5.

[59] Soltis, "Images of Justice," 115.

which public attention focused on the sentencing of Ma'lik Richmond and Trent Mays. In both the Bundy and Steubenville cases, the primary concern in determining if justice had been served was "to determine what the offender deserves," based upon guilt or innocence.[60] The docuseries *When They See Us* depicts this through the character of Linda Fairstein, the former head of the New York City sex crimes unit, and her efforts to convict Salaam, Richardson, Wise, Santana, and McCray at all costs.[61] The single story appears not only in terms of content, but also with respect to whose story is shared.

As Lyndsie and I have illustrated in Chapters 2 and 5, true crime predominantly tells the stories of white people from white perspectives, in which violence is gruesome and random. One rarely hears about transgender persons, migrant workers, or Indigenous people. True crime does not show the difficulties returning citizens have finding work and affordable housing. True crime covers up the ways in which mass incarceration has removed an entire generation of grandfathers from a community. True crime does not show us that the prison population is aging, and that access to healthcare is increasingly becoming an issue. True crime hides our failures to come up with better solutions to poverty, sexual abuse, mental illness, and child abuse. And what is most disconcerting about true crime media is the way it discourages an ethic of critical questioning and authentic discernment by hiding the brokenness of our humanity.

In *Just Mercy*, Bryan Stevenson talks about how his own proximity to the brokenness of others "exposed my own brokenness. You cannot effectively fight abusive power, poverty, inequality,

---

[60] Ibid., 114.

[61] See Susan Welsh, Keren Schiffman, and Enjoli Francis, "'I So Wish the Case Hadn't Been Settled': 1989 Central Park Jogger Believes More Than One Person Attacked Her," *ABC News*, May 23, 2019.

illness, oppression or injustice and not be broken by it."[62] Everyone is broken by something. The question that Stevenson asks
readers to reckon with is whether we are willing to embrace
our own brokenness or whether we try to hide it. We live in a
society that encourages us to hide brokenness—we hide broken
people by walking away from them or by hiding them out of
sight in institutions like prisons and nursing homes. We hide the
brokenness of lynching by whitewashing history and denying
the existence of racism, LGBTQ violence, ableism, and sexual
violence within our workplaces. We hide the brokenness of
white insecurities and white shame through the social construct
of niceness, in which BIPOC scholars are supposed to "temper
their anger and calmly educate" their white colleagues on racist,
sexist, and homophobic topics when asked.[63] Privileged groups
and institutions hide brokenness by refusing to acknowledge the
past, to apologize, or to work to repair relationships.

True crime media sends the message that it is okay not only
to hide brokenness, but to exploit people for profit. Journalist
Channing Gerard Joseph calls "on all American news organizations—including TV, radio, and social media outlets—to investigate, acknowledge, apologize, and make amends for their role in
disseminating racist ideas and profiting from racist violence."[64] As
Joseph points out, apologies are rare within the media industry,
and the few that do exist are often riddled with excuses. A good
apology names the harm done, is addressed to the appropriate
person (rather than using general or generic language), and is

---

[62] Bryan Stevenson, *Just Mercy: A Story of Justice and Redemption* (New York:
One World, 2015), 289.

[63] Colin Ben, Amber Poleviyuma, Jeremiah Chin, Alexus Richmond, Megan
Tom, and Sarah Abuwandi, "The Self-Contained Scholar: The Racialized
Burdens of Being Nice in Higher Education," in *The Price of Nice: How Good
Intentions Maintain Educational Inequity*, ed. Angelina Castagno (Minneapolis:
University of Minnesota Press, 2019), 146.

[64] Channing Gerard Joseph, "American Journalism's Role in Promoting
Racist Terror," *The Nation* (April 19, 2021), 31.

not defensive. In other words, the apology is not about making yourself look good.[65]

TAKING ACTION

What should white people do about this? First of all, we can allow ourselves to be uncomfortable. As Bryan Massingale advises: "Sit in the discomfort this hard truth brings. Let it become agonizing. Let it move you to tears, to anger, to guilt, to shame, to embarrassment. Over what? Over your ignorance."[66] Over the times that you took comfort in the single story that true crime propagates on air and on TV; over the times that you locked your car doors or clutched your purse when in the presence of darker bodies; over the times that you posted photos of yourself protesting on social media because deep down you wanted affirmation of your own goodness; over the times that you minimized a racist or sexist incident in your workplace because dealing with the conflict would just take too much energy and you "don't have that kind of time."

Letting yourself feel uncomfortable does not mean that white people always need to share their discomfort in public and with people of color. Recall the situation of the white board member described at the beginning of this chapter. As Collins and Jun suggest, and I agree, "White pain claims should be suspended when listening to accounts of racial injustice, even if the initial instinct is to try and share something similar. Listening, lamenting, and grieving are communal ways of hearing pain instead of making claims and stealing pain."[67] White pain can instead be

---

[65] Consider the response of the editor of the *Baltimore Sun*, which minimizes the harm done and points out that newspaper's accomplishments. See Paul Zieber, "A Newspaper Apologizes for Slave-Era Ads," *New York Times*, July 6, 2000. In contrast, the *Boston Globe* has teamed up with Boston University to dedicate a new publication toward racial justice, *The Emancipator.*

[66] Massingale, "White Privilege."

[67] Collins and Jun, *White Out*, 31.

expressed in white affinity groups or among friends and family. Making the shift to communal ways of hearing and expressing pain is critically important in challenging public understandings of racism. For to understand the term *racist* as a personal insult or character attack is to fail to interpret the structural nature of racism.[68] White desires to maintain moral goodness arise out of individualistic and dualistic interpretations of racism. I am a racist = I am a bad person; therefore, I must do something to prove that I am good. Other such binaries include: racist = evil; nonracist = innocent; racist = oppressor; and non-racist = victim. Such dualisms make it difficult for white feminists and white survivors of sexual violence to embrace the role that our whiteness plays in the violation of others.

History has been written in ways that define white women as victims. This is not honest. White women are not just victims; white women are also perpetrators and bystanders to sexual violence. White culture has also exploited BIPOC sexuality.[69] Women condemn each other, slut shaming those who defy traditional gender norms. As illustrated in Chapter 4, the point is that sexual violence cannot be understood apart from race and colonization. Many religious communities still struggle to talk about both sex and race in healthy ways. Therefore, sex education must include conversation about consent and race. Adolescents of all races should know who Emmett Till was and how ideas about race continue to shape contemporary discourse on sex in the media and beyond.[70] And adults need to know this, too. More

---

[68] Srivastava, "You're Calling Me a Racist?," 46.

[69] See Kelly Brown Douglas, *Sexuality and the Black Church: A Womanist Perspective* (Maryknoll, NY: Orbis Books, 1999), 125; and Rita Nakashima Brock, "Cooking without Recipes: Interstitial Integrity," in *Off the Menu: Asian and Asian North American Women's Religion and Theology*, ed. Rita Nakashima Brock, Jung Ha Kim, Kwok Pui-lan, and Seung Ai Yang, 125–44 (Louisville, KY: Westminster John Knox, 2007).

[70] See "Emmett Till's Murder, and How America Remembers Its Darkest Moments," *New York Times*, September 9, 2020.

work needs to be done at the local and parish level. One place to start would be broad implementation and creative interpretation of the work of BIPOC scholars within curricula and ministry.[71]

Second, white Christians need to begin to see race work as life work. Pay attention to whose voices you hear and why, both in the media and in your own relationships. How do you spend your time and why? While it might not seem like much, some of the most important conversations that can be had right now are in your own home, among your friends, and within faith communities. It takes a lot of courage, creativity, and persistence to find ways to talk to people that you see every day about policing, whiteness, criminalizing, sexual violence, and justice. These are not one-time conversations—they are ongoing conversations that require a conversion of heart and conversion to one another. It is difficult to develop relationships with those with whom we vehemently disagree. However, privileged people are responsible for the Karens of our workplaces, parent-teacher organizations, and neighborhoods. We are responsible for finding ways to convey the message that racist, sexist, and transphobic behavior will not be tolerated. It is the responsibility of privileged people to refuse to tolerate sexual harassment, micro-aggressions, and ableism in the workplace.

Third, become media literate. You cannot do this work without learning about the complexities of history. The Equal Justice Initiative, for example, has great resources available for people of all ages. Go to the Rosa Parks Museum in Montgomery, Alabama, or visit the Birmingham Civil Rights Insititute. Talk to your kids about what they watch. You might ask: How many white characters are there? How many BIPOC characters? Which character do you feel sorry for and why? What is the

---

[71] See, for example, Traci C. West, "Ending Gender Violence: An Antiracist Intersectional Agenda for Churches," *Review and Expositor* 117, no. 2 (2020): 199–203.

major conflict, and how is it resolved? As Massingale and others have argued, we have to reeducate ourselves. A critical task within this process involves parenting. Given the substantive amount of time today that people (including children) spend on their devices, do not underestimate the importance of media literacy within the work of racial justice. As the parent of a "tween" girl, I am well aware that I cannot control my child's media exposure. However, I can teach her how to evaluate critically what she is exposed to and to understand the complicated relationship that people have with technology today. Technology and media will always be changing; this is why media literacy is an ongoing moral project. You can also watch age-appropriate films that tell stories that have not yet been shared. There are a number of great documentaries and movies available that can help with the process of relearning. (*Just Mercy, Thirteenth, 4 Little Girls, I Am Evidence, I Learn America*, and *Living Undocumented* are all great places to start.) And do your research. Pay attention to what is happening in your own community. How many white people live on your street? Who and what is given priority in your local school district? Whom do you spend your time with socially?

Fourth, use your political power to bring about God's "kin-dom." All of us are endowed with moral agency. The question becomes, how are you going to use your agency? How are you going to show up in this world? At the very least, take the time to be an educated voter in local and national elections and work to ensure access for everyone to the polls on election day. This could be something as simple as making sure that people in your neighborhood have a ride to the polls. Also, take some time to get to know your neighbors and the local businesses in your neighborhood. Find out what is going on behind the scenes by developing concrete relationships with people. And for those of us who are theologians, ministers, and educators, it is past time for regular, systematic investigations of racial bias within our own institutions.

In the summer of 2020, a number of national theological and religious organizations including the board of directors of the Catholic Theological Society of America (CTSA) and the board of directors of the College Theology Society (CTS) released statements condemning racism, acknowledging complicity, and making a commitment to work to do better.[72] In full disclosure, I sat on the board of directors at the time the CTS statement was released. I do believe that solidarity statements are important, but they have to be followed by concrete action and data. The problem is not just "out there." Racism, heterosexism, and trans-phobia exist within the very walls of the institutions in which we work, educate, and worship. While some of this has already begun, we have a long way to go. Statements hold meaning only insofar as they are backed up by resources, strategic plans, and accountability. To my white colleagues, perhaps, this is our White-22. The next time we feel tempted to issue a statement on matters of race, let us take Collins and Jun's advice and sit down and listen first.

CONCLUDING THOUGHTS

In this book, we've provided plenty of different topics for reflection. But at the end of the day, it is up to you—you have to be willing to do the work of self-confrontation, to enter your own "racial crucible."[73] No one can do this for you. White people have a really hard time admitting that we are wrong. We often feel threatened. Look at how Amy Cooper responded when

---

[72] See CTSA Board of Directors, "Statement on "Racial Injustice and State Violence," June 3, 2020, ctas-online.org; and CTS Board of Directors, College Theology Society Board of Director's Statement on US Racism," May 30, 2020, collegetheology.org.

[73] Karen Teel, "The Racial Crucible: The Movement for Black Lives as Spiritual Invitation," *Critical Theology* 3, no 1 (2020): 7–14.

Christian Cooper reminded her that she needed to follow the park rules. As we noted in Chapter 4, for most white adults in this country the moral problem is not lack of awareness of white racism; the moral problem is failure to reverse the course of history. White supremacists and white liberals know that white racism exists. The difference is that white supremacists are willing to acknowledge their collusion with anti-Blackness. As Stevenson asks:

> I began to wonder what would happen if we all just acknowledged our brokenness, if we owned up to our weakness, our deficits, our biases, our fears. Maybe if we did, we wouldn't want to kill the broken among us who have killed others. Maybe we would look harder for solutions to caring for the disabled, the abused, the neglected, the traumatized.[74]

At the end of the day you have to be willing to make a long-term commitment to social transformation.

And while "racial justice movements are not dependent on white people for success," white people must still take responsibility for our white selves.[75] Saying that white people can do nothing leaves white people off the hook. And though white people should not be the leaders in antiracist movements, we do have a responsibility to participate, both individually and socially. As Bryan Massingale has argued, "To create a different world, we have to learn how this one came to be. And unlearn what we previously took for granted."[76] And while it doesn't seem glamorous or exciting, white people need to start debunking the implicit messages that are conveyed through the media about

---

[74] Stevenson, *Just Mercy*, 291.
[75] Sullivan, *Good White People*, 2.
[76] Massingale, "White Privilege."

racialized bodies, crime, and justice. This work is tedious and it is a long-term commitment. Yet, working for racial justice and gender justice is not about "earning points"; it is a lifelong process of conversion. The sooner white Christians can understand this, the better off we all will be.

Justice is about restoring right relationships, or about building a foundation for right relations to be established. It is never too late to rewrite the story of your life; neither is it too early to begin to repair relationships with the people in your life. The right time is now. But justice cannot be accomplished if we fail to honestly reckon with the brokenness in our midst. Only then can we find new kinds of stories to tell with our lives. What kind of story will your life tell?

EPILOGUE

Central to Christian teaching is the notion that human beings are created for relationship with God and one another. We need each other to thrive and survive in this world. Yet, we continue to live in a society that exacts justice through isolation and separation by depriving people of human contact. Exacting punishment by means of isolation is not justice. We recognize what is most essential for human survival, but we dehumanize by creating barriers to accessing it or by removing access to it altogether.

This reality really hit home to me the first time I (Elisabeth) walked into a maximum-security prison, at SCI Graterford, Pennsylvania (now closed), in the summer of 2014 as a part of the Inside-Out Prison Exchange instructor training program.[1] It was the first time I had ever met a person serving a life sentence, and I was surprised and humbled by his grasp of metaphysical philosophy. Most important, it was also the first time that I truly understood how vulnerable human beings are in the carceral system. That vulnerability affects not only those who are serving time, but equally so all who participate in the system. That summer I came to understand that my white racialized body

---

[1] The Inside-Out Prison Exchange Program is housed at Temple University. According to the program's website, "Inside-Out courses bring together traditional college students and incarcerated students in jails and prisons for semester long learning." For more, visit https://www.insideoutcenter.org/.

was integral to the operation of the US carceral system in both big and small ways.

Within the carceral system, contact with other civilians is a reward for good behavior, while isolation is punishment for behaving badly. Sadly, this form of punishment continues long after a person reenters society, as having a criminal record blocks access to housing, employment, and other avenues for participation in society.[2] I came to realize that violence within the US carceral system is predicated upon a deep recognition of the common humanity of those incarcerated.[3] The only reason it makes sense to punish people in the form of extreme isolation, and then to offer human contact as an incentive for improved behavior, is if you are able to recognize what companionship means to all people. Relationships humanize and restore dignity. In the context of the carceral system (as well as in other contexts of violence), the purposeful, systematic, long-term removal of healthy relationships requires the recognition of our shared common humanity. Therefore, to posit the mere recognition of our common humanity as a solution or part of the solution to criminal injustice and racial violence is to misconstrue the very nature of the violence itself. The moral problem, with respect to racism, is not simply the failure to recognize our common humanity or human dignity. The problem is far greater: it is the failure of our moral imagination. As Kelly Brown Douglas states, "Faith recognizes that God acts first, thus inviting human beings into a relationship. . . . This invitation comes in the form of God acting in the world to make real the freedom of God, which is love and life."[4] Therefore, human beings must work out our

---

[2] David Harris, "#131 Re-Entry: The Real Experience," podcast, *Criminal (In)Justice,* February 9, 2021.

[3] This realization was inspired in part from reading Kate Manne, *Down Girl: The Logic of Misogyny* (New York: Oxford University Press, 2017), 168.

[4] Kelly Brown Douglas, *Stand Your Ground: Black Bodies and the Justice of God* (Maryknoll, NY: Orbis Books, 2016), 224.

salvation in concert with God and in concert with other people as we work toward bringing about God's "kin-dom" on earth. In contexts marked by sustained, systemic injustice and violence, this work requires a radical moral imagination that is "grounded in the absolute belief that the world can be better."[5] Too many white Christians simply cannot imagine anything greater than the worlds we create for ourselves alone.

---

[5] Ibid., 225.

ACKNOWLEDGMENTS

When we first began this project, the world was a very different place. We did not know what 2020 and beyond were going to bring. To the many people who have walked with us throughout this journey, you have taught us what community feels like during a pandemic. We are grateful for family, friends, colleagues, and community members who encouraged, inspired, and challenged us in ways big and small. This project is dedicated to you. You have graced our lives in ways beyond measure.

This book started as a teaching collaboration that would engage students in moral reflection and scientific analysis using true crime media as an entry point, but it turned into so much more. We would like to thank our students in the spring 2021 class entitled "True Crime and the Justice of God" (at Duquesne University) for challenging and inspiring us along the way.

To the members of the Elsinore-Bennu Think Tank for Restorative Justice and the Voices for Juvenile Justice, thank you for welcoming us into your gracious space. Your authenticity and courage have inspired us to live deeper and bolder. A special thank you to Jamar Williams, who agreed to co-teach with us in the spring of 2021. We are more authentic and compassionate educators because of your wisdom.

Our colleagues have been an invaluable source of friendship and support throughout this project. Josh Ellsworth, Thomas

Farrell, Frederick Fochtman, Katie Grimes, Sharon Higginbo-tham, Jennifer Owens-Jofré, Missy Meredith, Morga Mihok, Joyce Sed, and Karen Teel have been particularly helpful in reading chapters of the manuscript, providing us with references, and/or thinking through the material with us. We also wish to thank Tim Frazier. Without his editing assistance, this manuscript would surely be less clear. We also wish to extend our gratitude to our colleagues at Duquesne University in the Department of Theology and the Forensic Science and Law Program.

We are sincerely grateful to all of the folks at Orbis Books who helped to bring this book to fruition, especially Jill Brennan O'Brien. She is the kind of editor who embodies an expansive moral imagination, bringing out the best in the writer and the project.

I, Lyndsie, want to thank my family and friends for your unending love, support, and encouragement. I am incredibly grateful for all the things you do to show you care. Thank you to my parents, David and Sherri, for loving me unconditionally and supporting my work. To my in-laws, Rudy and Patty, for the endless encouragement and love. To my sister Alyssa and her family, Patrick, Maddox, and Mila, for always checking in and brightening my mood. To my grandparents, Sharon, Joanne, and Ed, for always cheering me on and celebrating the journey. A special thank you to Michael, my partner. I would be lost with-out your unwavering love and support. While writing this book and navigating the pandemic you lifted me up, kept me balanced, and allowed me to recognize the joy surrounding us.

Elisabeth, I am incredibly grateful to call you a coauthor, col-league, and friend. Thank you for trusting in me and believing in this collaboration. Through this experience you've taught me so much. I'm extremely grateful that you pushed me outside of my comfort zone, challenged me to dig deeper, and always believed in me even when I doubted myself. You continually inspire me with your depth of knowledge, profound compassion, and dedication to those you love. I am a better scholar, educator, and person because of you. I'm excited for what the future holds.

And I, Elisabeth, wish to thank my family and friends, who have always been my cheerleaders, celebrating my accomplishments and loving me when I stumble and fall. To my parents, Michael and Therese, thank you for reading chapters and spending time with Elise over Zoom. To Scott, your support and friendship mean the world to me (and so did the meals and childcare!). This book could not have been completed otherwise. Finally, Elise—this book is for you. You are my greatest delight! I am so proud of the person that you are becoming: smart, passionate, and beautiful. May you learn from your mistakes, see the beauty in yourself and others, and continue to seek justice in the world.

Lyndsie, I am grateful for you. Writing has always been a lonely experience for me. I never felt alone in this book. You have challenged me to grow not only as a scholar, but as a human being. You stretched my understanding of what interdisciplinary and collaborative scholarship could mean in the classroom and beyond. I could not have asked for a better colleague and friend. I am honored and graced to be a part of the many people that you call home. I am excited about our future adventures!

INDEX